Spencer

Walking
Backwards

FARRAR, STRAUS AND GIROUX   NEW YORK

*Walking
Backwards*

*Poems
1966–2016*

*John
Koethe*

Farrar, Straus and Giroux

120 Broadway, New York 10271

Grateful acknowledgment is made for permission to reprint the following material: Eleven poems from The Late Wisconsin Spring by John Koethe. Copyright © 1984 by John Koethe. Reprinted by permission of Princeton University Press. Nine poems from The Constructor by John Koethe. Copyright © 1999 by John Koethe. Reprinted by permission of HarperCollins Publishers. Nine poems from Falling Water by John Koethe. Copyright © 1997 by John Koethe. Reprinted by permission of HarperCollins Publishers. Thirteen poems from North Point North: New and Selected Poems by John Koethe. Copyright © 2002 by John Koethe. Reprinted by permission of HarperCollins Publishers. Eleven poems from Sally's Hair: Poems by John Koethe. Copyright © 2006 by John Koethe. Reprinted by permission of HarperCollins Publishers. Twelve poems from Ninety-Fifth Street by John Koethe. Copyright © 2009 by John Koethe. Reprinted by permission of HarperCollins Publishers. Twelve poems from ROTC Kills by John Koethe. Copyright © 2012 by John Koethe. Reprinted by permission of HarperCollins Publishers.

The Library of Congress has cataloged the hardcover edition as follows:

Names: Koethe, John, 1945– author.

Title: Walking backwards : poems, 1966–2016 / John Koethe.

Description: First edition. | New York : Farrar, Straus and Giroux, 2018. |

Includes index.

Identifiers: LCCN 2018019109 | ISBN 9780374285791 (hardcover)

Classification: LCC PS3561.O35 A6 2018 | DDC 811/.54—dc23

LC record available at https://lccn.loc.gov/2018019109

Paperback ISBN: 978-0-374-53870-5

Designed by Quemadura

TO DIANE

A NOTE ON CHRONOLOGY

Some of the poems in *Domes* (1973) were first published in book form in *Blue Vents* (1968). Those that I have chosen to reprint here are included in the selections from *Blue Vents*.

Both *Falling Water* (1997) and *The Constructor* (1999) comprise poems written between 1985 and 1996, arranged into two books along broadly thematic lines. Though *The Constructor* was published after *Falling Water*, the poems in it are on average earlier than the poems in the latter book, and to reflect this I have placed the selections from *The Constructor* before those from *Falling Water*.

CONTENTS

New Poems

*Walking
Backwards*

ENGLISH 206

Why would anyone even want to do it anymore?
Fifty-two years ago I didn't know what it was,
And yet I knew I wanted to do it too, like the idea of a mind
The self aspires to, the self a mind endeavors to become.

I still don't and still do. Yeats and Frost, Pound and Eliot,
Stevens, Moore, seen as from a peak in Darien in a college course
With a syllabus, lectures twice a week, a final exam—
It might not sound transformative, but in an incidental way

What I am now, what I'll die as, and how I'll linger on
For the small while that constitutes an afterlife
Was there from the first day: the urgency, the anxiety,
The sense of something insisting to be said

Again, before the mystery and necessity drifted away.
It looks different now. What's become of poetry
Are different kinds of poets, i.e., different kinds of people
Having nothing much in common but the name.

I miss the echo chamber, where you studied to become
Something unforeseen, recognizable in retrospect.
I miss the mystery, the feeling of history gradually unfolding
And the way it made no sense at all until it did.

In the afternoon of the author everything is there to see.
No one told me when I was starting out "that day so long ago"
That things become more and more familiar, then suddenly you're old,
With nothing to do and nothing stretching out before you

To infinity, reducing whatever you did or had to say
To a footnote, skipped over in the changing afternoon light,
That finally becomes, at best, part of the narrative
In a MoMA of the mind. But I'm glad I did it anyway.

2017

Blue Vents

(1968)

YOUR DAY

I've spent the whole day listening
to you, or looking for paintings
                              with you, the one
I finally bought has a girl in a yellow
dress standing next to a white wall
that looks like cheese
                      I carried it
home under my jacket, it was raining
                                   you stumbled
and caught your balance I think
my Italian cookbook is all nonsense
you move beautifully riding the subway
or bending to put on a record
                            when you sing
hold the microphone, sing into it
                                I say
over drinks in a dark room
                          your ears look red
in front of the lamp
I am sleepy, the record seems louder
            everything is moving

MONTANA

I get lost in your dresses. The grace
You enlist as you join me
In the room that is smaller than both of us
Is emptier than you are and more part of us.

I wish you were a long movie—
Surprising as goodness, humorless, and really unclever.
I think of the places you'd visit.
I think of what you'd be like in a "context."

And I feel like a saucer of milk
Or a car with its lights on in daylight.
For the day will accept us without noise

And your noise that is shaped like sound never changes.
And I can hear it, but like a screen

It divides me
It makes you stay where you are.
At home we could understand pictures
That enlarged as you became part of them,

That enlarged as you vanished into them, my stories
Were all about trains with an outline of horses

And they were real trains. So my thoughts of you move
Over all we've deliberately forgotten.
And our luck is all still out there.

MAPS

Maps are a guide to good conduct.
They will not go away from your life,
But in return, they promise you safety
And entertain you with political visions.

As investments in the commonplace
The cowboy and mystic alike both need trains—
Formulaic, impersonal trains,
Warmed by the engineer's tears.

Theirs is a history of polite good sense
Yet it has the perfect confidence of a dream.
Now nothing can alter your body,
But the dream changes when you go away

And information arises to take its place.
Carried from place to arrival,
Operating on a program of intense change,
You seem a part of the lives of those near you

But the horizon is made of expensive steel
That dopes you with a sort of elastic energy
Like a particular spot in the brain.
He is a precision-made man

Whose life is a series of privileged instants,
Examples—like greeting or going away.
But who can remember old entertainment?
The couple locked in a good hotel,

The hotel locked with a profound happiness.
Outside, the forest. These maps
Prevent sadness, but really are nothing but history
Of simple encounter, or dreams and geometrical charms.

They are samples. They move in the light.
The light continues to move in the eye
Of a sleeping man. A tremendous hint
Falls over the station: the man is about to be killed.

At best he will be permitted to live in an old mine.
The girl evaporates in back of a city official
And in the mirror the boy holds up his hands
To cover his face. Anyway, nobody comes.

Where are the acts you tried to conceal
Like a hand you put away somewhere and forgot?
The spirit died when the man went into the cave
But see what these maps have done with your hand.

PROCESS

Like that definite thing
I'd postponed, calling you
The sky's clear streak facing
The porch—how can my emotions be
So thin, and so lately recognized?
You remind me. Chords of you slumber fitfully

Tossing the bottled logic swans and
Imperial necks, vases, counterpoints
The lightning silent but "edgy."
This room must have a past,
I am living in it.
Here the rain though discontinued
Comes out like thunder—that baffles
You, and your innocence that I invent.

LEVEL

Eventually, I'd hoped, I would please you.
I would call you the right names,
Bend with your gestures, remember your actions,
Extracting them gladly, but within real limits.

I see I was wrong. Shall I find you different,
Easy, supple, and without pain?
Or is energy part of the music?
I try. I am trying to ask you.

O the noises that cannot be touched!
The faces have passed me like a brown dream

For how can they change?
Always unbearably tender, and constant,
Like a house that is tender and constant.

You are like other people. There is,
I suppose, no reason to want you
Unless desire itself is a reason, drawing us
Out of our kindness, leaving us terrified

Peace. Beauty, we know,
Is the center of fear, hammering,
Holding in a loose ring your purposeful
Dream—and you see them

Looking painfully into your face, though you know
They will never come back in the same way.

BIRD

What bird has read *all* the books?
The crow lives by a passionate insincerity
That means naturalness in an impossible world

And so is a unit by which we can measure ourselves
In the real one. The swallow defines "exact place"
So that we know it exists beyond sight

And the criminal depth of the night sky.
Yet owls never move, flamingos just
Stand there, victims of the tall trees

And emblems of space or beautiful hair.
Our little canary recalls the first crisis:
Inclined planes, the separate enterprises

Necessary if we are able to exist at all.
The birds cannot reach us.
But we hear the sleeping art of their music

And it hints at all the evaporated experience
We need for our simplest move, our first
Aspiration, "flight." Hummingbirds are just space.

Domes

(1973)

SONG

I used to like getting up early
(I had to anyway) when the light was still smoky
And before the sun had finished burning the fog away.
The sun rose behind a cool yellow mountain

I could see through my window, and its first rays
Hit a funny-looking bump on the wall next to my head.
I would look at it for a little while and then get up.
Meanwhile, something was always doing in the kitchen,

For every day took care of itself:
It was what I got dressed for, and then it moved away
Or else it hung around waiting for someone to turn
Saying "I thought so." But it always ended.

—I know it's hopeless remembering,
The memories only coming to me in my own way, floating around like
    seeds on the wind
Rustling in the leaves of the eucalyptus tree each morning,
The texture of light and shade. They feel the same, don't they,

All these memories, and each day seems,
Like one in high school, a distraction from itself
Prefaced only by one of a few dreams, resembling each other
Like parts of the same life, or like the seasons.

Come spring you'd see lots of dogs
And summer was the season when you got your hair cut off.
It rained a little more in winter, but mostly,
Like autumn, one season resembled the next

And just sat there, like the mountain with the "S" on it,
Through weather every bit as monotonous as itself.
And so you'd lie in bed, wondering what to wear that day,
Until the light mended and it was time to get ready for school.

—Is there anything to glean from these dumb memories?
They let you sleep for a while, like Saturday,
When there was nothing you were supposed to do.
But it doesn't seem enough just to stay there,

Close to the beginning,
Rubbing your eyes in the light, wondering what to wear now, what to say:
Like the eternal newcomer with his handkerchief and his lunchpail,
Looking around, and then sliding away into the next dream.

BELOW THE COAST

A clumsy hillock
Unmolded like a cake on the meadow
In the Laguna Mountains. Tough yellow-green grass growing up to a tree
As thick as a tooth. In winter, on the road from San Diego,
Thousands of cars crawl up to the snow
And their passengers get out to investigate it
And then drive, discoursing, back home. And that's California,
Solemnly discharging its responsibilities.

Meanwhile we breakfast on pancakes the size of a plate
While the console radio goes on the blink.
Miss L'Espagnole looks out from her frame on the wall,
Completely prepared (though for what it is impossible to say).
Her left arm is white and dips into a puddle of fire
Or a pile of cotton on fire. And each thing is severe:
The house hemmed in by pepper trees and Mexico
(This one is white and in Chula Vista), and the paraphernalia
Strewn around home: a few magazines summing up politics,
A matchbox with a lavender automobile on the cover,
And a set of soldiers of several military epochs marching off to war on
    the raffia rug.
Unless you've grown up amidst palm trees (and buildings that are either
    unbuilt, or hospitals)
It's impossible to appreciate a reasonable tree.

   I sometimes consider the parrots that live in the zoo
   And are sold on the street in Tijuana. Colored like national flags,
   Their heads are always cocked to pick up something behind them.

And unless you have lived in a place where the fog
Closes in like a face, it is impossible to be (even temporarily) relieved
When it lifts to expose the freshly painted trim of the city, and it seems
Like a fine day for knowledge: sunlight sleeping on top of the rocks
And lots of white clouds scudding by like clean sheets,
Which, when the air in the bedroom is cold, you pull over your head
And let the temperature slowly increase while you breathe.
But California has only a coast in common with this.

DOMES

FOR JOHN GODFREY

1. ANIMALS

Carved—indicated, actually—from solid
Blocks of wood, the copper-, cream-, and chocolate-colored
Cows we bought in Salzburg form a tiny herd.
      And in Dr. Gachet's etching, six
Or seven universal poses are assumed by cats.

Misery, hypocrisy, greed: a dying
Mouse, a cat, and a flock of puzzled blackbirds wearing
Uniforms and frock coats exhibit these traits.
      Formally outlasting the motive
Of their creation with a poetry at once too vague

And too precise to do anything with but
Worship, they seem to have just blundered into our lives
By accident, completely comprehending
      Everything we find so disturbing
About them; but they never speak. They never even move

From the positions in which Grandville or some
Anonymous movie-poster artist has left them,
A sort of ghostly wolf, a lizard, an ape
      And a huge dog. And their eyes, looking
At nothing, manage to see everything invisible

To ours, even with all the time in the world
To see everything we think we have to see. And tell
Of this in the only way we really can:
            With a remark as mild as the air
In which it is to be left hanging; or a stiff scream,

Folded like a sheet of paper over all
The horrible memories of everything we were
Going to have. That vanished before our eyes
            As we woke up to nothing but these,
Our words, poor animals whose home is in another world.

2. SUMMER HOME

Tiny outbursts of sunlight play
On the tips of waves that look like tacks
Strewn upon the surface of the bay.
Up the coast the water backs up
Behind a lofty, wooded island. Here,
According to photographs, it is less
Turbulent and blue; but much clearer.
It seems to exercise the sunlight less
Reflecting it, allowing beaten silver sheets
To roam like water across a kitchen floor.
Having begun gradually, the gravel beach
Ends abruptly in the forest on the shore.

Looked at from a distance, the forest seems
Haunted. But safe within its narrow room

Its light is innocent and green, as though
Emerging from another dream of diminution
We found ourselves of normal, human size,
Attempting to touch the leaves above our heads.
Why couldn't we have spent our summers here,
Surrounded and growing up again? Or perhaps
Arrive here late at night by car, much later
In life? If only heaven were not too near
For such sadness. And not within this world
Which heaven has finally made clear.

Green lichen fastened to a blue rock
Like a map of the spot; cobwebs crowded with stars
Of water; battalions of small white flowers.
Such clarity, unrelieved except by our
Delight and daily acquiescence in it,
Presumably the effect of a natural setting
Like this one, with all its expectations of ecstasy
And peace, demands a future of forgetting
Everything that sustains it: the dead leaves
Of winter; the new leaves of spring which summer burns
Into different kinds of happiness; for these,
When autumn drops its tear upon them, turn.

3. DOMES

"Pleased in proportion to the truth
Depicted by means of familiar images." That
One was dazed; the other I left in a forest

Surrounded by giant, sobering pines.
For I had to abandon those lives.
Their burden of living had become
Mine and it was like dying: alone,
Huddled under the cold blue dome of the stars,
Still fighting what died and so close to myself I could not even see.
I kept trying to look at myself. It was like looking into the sun and I went
    blind.

O to break open that inert light
Like a stone and let the vision slowly sink down
Into the texture of things, like a comb flowing through dark,
Heavy hair; and to continue to be affected much later.
I was getting so tired of that excuse: refusing love
Until it might become so closely mated to its birth in
Acts and words of love; until a soft monstrosity of song
Might fuse these moments of affection with a dream of home;
The cold, prolonged proximity of God long after night
Has come and only starlight trickles through the dome;
And yet I only wanted to be happy.

I wanted rest and innocence; a place
Where I could hide each secret fear by blessing it,
By letting it survive inside those faces I could never understand,
Love, or bear to leave. Because I wanted peace, bruised with prayer
I tried to crawl inside the heavy, slaughtered hands of love
And never move. And then I felt the wound unfold inside me
Like a stab of paradise: explode: and then at last
Exhausted, heal into pain. And that was happiness:
A dream whose ending never ends, a vein

Of blood, a hollow entity
Consumed by consummation, bleeding so.
In the sky our eyes ascend to as they sweep
Upwards into emptiness, the angels sing their listless
Lullabies and children wake up glistening with screams
They left asleep; and the dead are dead. The wounded worship death
And live a little while in love; and then are gone.
Inside the dome the stars assume the outlines of their lives:
Until we know, until we come to recognize as ours,
Those other lives that live within us as our own.

TINY FIGURES IN SNOW

Cut out of board
And pinned against the sky like stars;
Or pasted on a sheet of cardboard
Like the small gold stars you used to get for being good:
Look at the steeple—
All lit up inside the snow
And yet without a single speck of snow on it.
The more I looked at it, the harder it became to see,
As though I tried to look at something cold
Through something even colder, and could not quite see.
And like the woman in the nursery rhyme
Who stared and stared into the snow until
She saw a diamond, shuddering with light, inside the storm,
I thought that we could see each snowflake wobble through the air
And hear them land.
Locked in her room
With yellow flowers on the wallpaper
That wove and welled around her like the snow
Until she almost disappeared in them,
Rapunzel in her cone let down the string the whole world could have
    climbed to save her.
"Oh, don't save me right away," Rapunzel said, "just visit me,"
But only dead ones listened to her.
Only the dead could ever visit us this way: locked in a word,
Locked in a world that we can only exorcise, but not convey.

SATIE'S SUITS

Orange is the hue of modernity.
Greater than gold, shaky and poetic,
Our century's art has been a gentle surrender
To this color's nonchalant "stance"

Towards hunger and the unknown, and its boldness:
For it has replaced us as the subject of the unknown.
We still like the same things, but today we handle them differently.
Among the signs of occupation in this contemporary war

The twelve identical corduroy suits of Erik Satie
Locate importance in repetition, where it really belongs,
There in the dark, among the lessons that sleep excludes.
I want to emphasize the contribution of each one of us

To a society which has held us back but which has
Allowed love to flourish in this age like a song.
Unable to understand very much,
But prepared to isolate things in a personal way,

The acres of orange paint are a sign
Of the machine that powers our amateur hearts.
The technical has been driven back
By river stages, exposing a vacant lot

Strewn with these tools, food and clothing
Awaiting the invention of limited strength.
We could begin selling ourselves, but the overture
Brings no response and the connection remains unsketched.

I can see there has been no change.
The body's a form of remote control
And its success is too exact to assist us.
Responding to the ulterior commandment

So much has failed in the abstract.
The phallus hid in the school bell
While the difficult fluid rose in the night.
In the apartment wild horses took you away.

POWER AND PERSUASION

June, its weejuns shoot below the trees.
I was scraping this paste out of my pajamas
Ready for graduation and the big green clot
Of June to come and get in touch with me.
A group of students disappeared in foliage at my feet.

O for a room furnished with a radio
And a complete set of *National Geographic* so I could grow up again.
As though I'd fallen through a telescope into the room
I felt oversized, too near the people, and their things surround me,
Like a child who feels older than he really wants to be.

SUMMER

It's a sooty disgrace—
Four city days of snow and now physics
Turning the page from white into black.
Sears' parking lot is finally open again
To cars from which people emerge only to falter
Headlong into ice and grime.

But can you imagine Boston blown open
Like a delicious orange promise, all wet
And deserving the pressure of our feet,
The hard details of love in the city
Amidst want and taxis, so bravely specific.

    I was going to say it's "enchanting"
    But I'm not sure now . . .
           this sleep—
           is it one of those "facts"
           of literature pulling us away from
           each other in the February dark?

It's so hard to remember the green,
The blue and ordinary persuasions of summer—
Nights that never seem to begin and then continue
Forever, the leaves dried out by the warm wind,
All the empirical information of a June day.
Even then, when the cold eases itself out of life

To fly in a few words into space, I guess some
People continue to dwell in their unremitting holes,
Blind to the reassurance of your face. But there
I find an understanding of love and drudgery
And coffee at seven o'clock in the morning, before
The day wraps us up in its pristine cares that bounce off
Into the cold winter air while under our skins
The small pleasures beat in our blood.

COPLEY SQUARE

Up-and-down shafts of light brick
Lift occupants up into prisms or roofs
Of green copper, and then embark on the sky.
12:44 by the Suffolk Franklin Savings Bank's
Clock, 93° outside, inside a cool bed of dimes.
A jet overhead that gets picked up by a pigeon
Gliding by lower down, some more modern banks
And a bank of lanterns set like a row of spears.
A Try Rooti Root Beer truck almost collides
With a spiffy yellow Checker Cab, and flags
Flop in front of the Sheraton Plaza Hotel.
Plenty of seersucker walks by below, or sits
On a deep-heated long granite bench,
Listening to the library,
Half-eating a half-eaten peach,
And bakes in the breeze.

THE HAND IN THE BREAST POCKET

1.

My first memory is of the house on Maxim Street
Where we lived in the early '50s.
There was a local haunted house
And a vacant lot where
Dale-girl, Dale-boy and I played on the monkey bars.
Dale-girl later swallowed a common household poison and had to
    have her stomach pumped.
I remember reading the encyclopedia a lot,
And dreaming of a man in a top hat with a toilet instead of a head.
I remember going to the drive-in wearing my pajamas
And falling asleep.
The first movie I remember seeing
Was *It Came from Outer Space*.

When I was about eight
We moved into a house with a green roof
And a lath house in the backyard.
It was close to the airport.
I remember lying in bed, listening to the television in the living room
And thinking that the airplanes flying overhead were Russian.
One Christmas I got a bicycle
Which I rode to the seamy side of town where most of the horror
    movies were,
And I had to take piano lessons from a nun who always said

"Hay is for horses"
Whenever I used the word "Hey!"
And I had a microscope,
A BB-gun,
One vicious dog and one kind dog.
When we moved away I kissed the house good-bye.

Our next house
—My last house—
Was on the edge of a huge canyon,
With a patio enclosed by sea-green fiberglass.
Manzanita bushes and ice-plant grew up to the garage.
It was 1957, the year of Sputnik,
And I conducted "science experiments" behind the garage,
I.e., set off rockets filled with a mixture of sulphur and zinc dust.
Once one of my friends set fire to part of the garage.
I remember taking clarinet lessons
And selling chocolate for the Cody Marching Band.
And reading *Tom Sawyer* and all the Sherlock Holmes stories over and
    over every year . . .

2.

Those are my favorite facts,
The facts of a life which now has virtually nothing to do with my own.
I wanted to feel the information flow through me like a prism,
To feel the light of everything I had ever done pass through me on its
    way to the rainbow.

This is not memory.

It's more like poking through the trash for something you threw away
  by mistake,

The clarity, the confusion,

The liquid years and now the ones which are like pills.

It's been a long day.

And there aren't any faces in this night,

No real names.

And now each day seems,

Like my own soul, farther and farther off,

Lost in its light as in a dream in which I meant to ask you something.

I can feel the life vibrating next to me.

But each day I wear the same clothes,

I say most of the same things,

Somebody listens to them

—Isn't there a moment all this is closing on,

Innocent enough to breathe,

A moment innocent enough to bear its own interpretation?

It's all so natural now,

Everything seems natural.

And I was going to tell you about everything I did today

Leaving none of them out,

The ones whose lives stop here

And about whom there is nothing to say, nothing to look forward to,

But now I'm not sure that they really exist,

The way I do, in time:

Time is what they do.

When I was ten I had this
Magic 8-Ball, filled with black ink
In which an octahedron floated, bearing my eight fortunes on its sides.
They were all useless and general;
But they were all true.
And they floated up to the window when I turned it over.

The Late
Wisconsin Spring

(1984)

DOROTHY WORDSWORTH

All my life
I've meant something I don't really know how to say—
Roughly, that *now* and *then* and *here* and *there*
Are different times and places, but not different ways of doing things;
And that every time and place is so dense
It can't hold any of the others,
But only sits next to them.
It's as though the "knowledge of experience"
Were that experience didn't matter all that much,
And that what I thought and meant and wanted
Didn't make very much difference, and that the past was a demonstration
Of how little weight the soul actually has.

And yet I still like most of the things
I used to like in high school, and I still think
Some of those wonderful, vague things are me.
I guess the things one has always liked
Don't have much to do with what one is, was, or ultimately becomes—
But I feel lost without them.
Fixed on something so far away my whole
Life seems prolonged out of proportion to the real world,
Things float in and stop and try to talk to me
And I agree with everything they say, though their voices aren't mine
    anymore:
It's getting awfully late. And we've all
Been up for a long time. In just a little while
All of us are going to be sound asleep.

Sometimes I can almost visualize my life
As a succession of those states—
Feelings of finitude, inklings of infinity
And the occasional breath of a human detail—
And it terrifies me to think that those moments could comprise
    everything I was ever actually going to feel.
But Dorothy Wordsworth went about her chores
In the throes of a dependency "so greatly loved
And so desperately clung to that it couldn't risk anything
But a description of the scenery in which it was lived";
And somehow accomplished her imagination.
And the long walks her brother took
In a phase of mind at one remove from description
Seem almost tangible now, and as funny and real
As the minutiae of real life.
Only they seem "absolutely small."

Puffy-lidded, doe-eyed,
With the detachment that characterizes
The fanatic, to whom nights and days are like children's stories
That don't explain anything but, taken together,
Make a fundamental kind of sense,
The sense of the mirror—
I thought I'd composed my life
Around a series of weightless moments,
And that each moment culminated in one of those remarks
People made at home, or overheard,
Or lost track of in a conversation,
And which were supposed to be as light as feathers.
But now I don't think anything like that ever really transpired at all.

EACH ONE AS SHE MAY

One life is enough. One private story
Lived out on a summer day. The play of the wind
And the fastidious vacuity of the mind
Lifting the chaos of emotion at the heart of life

Into these clouds of feeling, these reflections
Of the glancing voice upon the dark, unformulated sob.
The birds are singing and the mind is still.
This is how my life was always going to be.

But another time it might have quietly opened out
To take in all of the vulgar disarray
Sprawled out here under the uncomprehending sun.
A simplifying memory might have smiled and sighed

Because it knew its kind of happiness could never end
And that a moment of eternal recompense and peace
Lay in the cool sweetness of the summer shade.
But now the days go by and each one is the same

For life is reading and respite from reading,
And living in a vague idea of where the others are,
Or in dreams, or in these simple versions of the past.
So let the wind die and the birds fall silent

And the gladness of the summer afternoon dissolve
Into these light, distracted semblances of life
Drawn from a purely private story of unwritten grief
And happiness, for myself and strangers.

A LONG LESSON

FOR JOHN ASHBERY

I spent a summer growing in that dream.
I looked—each day a little differently—
At what was there, and put it down:
The child, the family, the pets,
The ones who really tried to pray to God,
And the others, who only stared at him
In disbelief, excused themselves, and left.
I slammed the kitchen door and went outside.
It was a nice day. The flowers waved at me.
The little leaves vibrated in the breeze.
I lay down on the lawn and went to sleep
But it was always the same dream: the house
Was full of strangers; they were calling me
To come inside, but finally were still.
It was quiet and the backyard started
Glowing like a magic garden, cold
And green and full of trees, and when I tried
To wake I only grew, until I woke up looking
Into someone else's eyes at what I was:
What I would always be, but blind.

Let him sleep. And let the others
Heal in their hate: I hid my heart.
The child bore me down without a word.
His art was gentle, his emotions were
As vague as hills, and his spirit stank,

But the pockets in the air he breathed between
Were my whole life. He gave me everything;
He forgave; he took the world away.

If I was a wall about myself, still
I knew I lived in heaven: quiet rooms
Full of pleasant furniture and lots of plants
And all day full of sunshine; and at night
The light of tiny steel stars. Only
There was another world—it was a wonderland
Of happiness and ruined homes, that even God
Could only look upon in suffering.
But it was mine. I tried to live in it.
I felt it sob inside me like a child.
Sometimes I thought I heard him calling me;
Sometimes I knew that I was only crying,
That he *was* the other life we shared
Before we grew: our little sacrament,
My tomb, my throne, my poor God's body
Broken on his world, a world he made and
Opened to the boy in innocence. And later,
When he became a man, I knew I was alone.

O let him know the hurt, the happiness
That separates the hunger and the fall,
O bring him home! But he never healed.
He was my home. He was the altar where
I worshipped what I was, and made it die:
The garden where he slept; the dingy room
Where he was practicing the piano;
His school uniform; the funny little shoes

He wore in paradise; his attitudes; his eyes
That stared me back across the sweet decay.
It wasn't that he was unhappy or
Unsatisfied or too satisfied or mean—
But that he never went away. He led me
Deeper in his dreams, until I thought
That I could live alone with what I knew:
That far beyond myself I was a boy;
And that he was all of heaven that I had.

Where is that world, the one I made
From prayers for its return, the world where God
Is slowly dying for us through eternity?
Even to see it is to see it fade.
How could we stand the slow love, or
Endure the solitude that might have freed us,
Or the certainty that should have made us
Happy to be free? Where all day long
We wandered back and forth below the huge trees
And when night came and the summer moon
Was motionless, stirred in our dreams, as though
Even the slightest motion would have made them real.
Could we ever bear to be so happy? But it died
And died in us so differently it almost
Seems I might have never needed you:
I might have never looked at you
Through eyes the same as yours, through tears.
Or was that happiness? I could have dreamed
All those other lives. Wasn't it enough to dream?

He might have lifted me through the leaves,
Over the houses where the hate was sleeping,
Through the sunlight; and I might have seen,
Immaculate with snow, the floating mountains
Limiting the world, a world so beautiful.
Poor seed—poor blind seed shed from heaven,
Swollen in the earth until it grew—
Our lives change. And our worlds, like dreams
So absolute even our sorrow seems
A form of happiness, are being changed.

KINDERSZENEN

Like that bird there, it alights and sings a song
And flies away again. And I don't want it to stay—
It's too early and I'm not quite ready for them yet:
I'm still thinking about them. And I know that the only true way is
    patience,
But if I could remember their names, remember what the trees looked
    like,
Or the details of that afternoon . . .
But a soft summer rain fell last night, and this morning the breeze was
    back.
It must have happened sometime during the night
Or early this morning while I was still sleeping,
And at first I didn't notice that anything had changed.
For I spend so much of my time alone,
Watching myself for the first, faint stirrings of a life
Which isn't mine anymore, and which I know can't be apprehended
    that way,
That sometimes the moments seem to lapse entirely inside me
On a transparent screen, or in a world where nothing real is ever
    going to happen.
Only this afternoon everything seemed changed: my friends weren't
    there,
But somehow it didn't bother me that nothing was ever going to bring
    them back again.
I kept listening to the wind: its purling sounded like time
Repeating something I'd been listening to for years, but hadn't had
    the character to say:

That they weren't real. That they'd only inhabited my imagination
Because it was empty. And that I didn't care what happened to them
    anymore.
For as I thought about them this afternoon
They began to seem weightless, and the oppressiveness of nearly twenty
    years
Seemed to fall away, leaving me alone in a small room
Trying to write a poem whose figures were unreal
Shadows cast by a single moment on the rest of time,
On the remainder of the world. After all, what were they
But the mirroring surface of a sob as it flooded a mind
Crammed full of useless details, like the traffic noises
Carried here on the wind, or something I said years ago,
One summer afternoon, to some friends whose names I can't even
    remember anymore.
It doesn't matter who they were. They kept me alive,
Protected from the others by a child's picture of what the world was like
Before they disappeared, like whole moments, back into time.

PARTIAL CLEARANCE

Barely a week later
I'd returned to myself again.
But where a light perspective of particulars
Used to range under an accommodating blue sky
There were only numb mind tones, thoughts clenched like little fists,
And syllables struggling to release their sense to my imagination.
I tried to get out of myself
But it was like emerging into a maze:
The buildings across the street still looked the same,
But they seemed foreshortened,
Dense, and much closer than I'd ever realized,
As though I'd only seen them previously in a dream.
Why is it supposed to be so important to see things as they actually are?
The sense of life, of what life is *like*—isn't that
What we're always trying so desperately to say?
And whether we live in between them,
Mirror each other out of thin air, or exist only as reflections
Of everything that isn't ours, we all sense it,
And we want it to last forever.

PICTURE OF LITTLE LETTERS

I think I like this room.
The curtains and the furniture aren't the same
Of course, but the light comes in the window as it used to
Late in the morning, after the others had gone to work.
You can even shave in it. On the dresser with the mirror
Are a couple of the pictures we took one afternoon
Last May, walking down the alley in the late sunlight.
I remember now how we held hands for fifteen minutes

Afterwards. The words meander through the mirror
But I don't want them now, I don't want these abbreviations.
What I want in poetry is a kind of abstract photography
Of the nerves, but what I like in photography
Is the poetry of literal pictures of the neighborhood.

The late afternoon sunlight is slanting through the window
Again, sketching the room in vague gestures of discontent
That roll off the mind, and then only seem to disappear.
What am I going to do now? And how am I going to sleep tonight?

A peculiar name flickers in the mirror, and then disappears.

MALIGNANT CALM

These things left in your hands,
Part calculation, part the unguarded effects
Of casual introspection, hormonal swings,
The close weather we've been having lately,
Aren't less human for what they hide, for what they
Mean without, somehow, ever quite managing to say—
Only weird, and sometimes just a little bit hard to absorb.
The eye glances through them and moves along, restlessly,
Like sunlight bouncing from wave to tiny wave,
Working the surface into an overall impression
Of serenity and mature reflection, a loose portrait
Of the face of early middle age. They are not meant
For anyone, yet reveal, like the tight corners of the mouth,
An intensity that overwhelms the things I wanted to say to you,
Blurring whatever it was that brought us together like this again,
Face to deflected face, shouting into the other as though it were a cave
And I drew my life from the echo of what I told you, from what you
    said to me.
Sometimes they even seem like enough, sufficient unto the day.

THE LATE WISCONSIN SPRING

Snow melts into the earth and a gentle breeze
Loosens the damp gum wrappers, the stale leaves
Left over from autumn and the dead brown grass.
The sky shakes itself out. And the invisible birds
Winter put away somewhere return, the air relaxes,
People start to circulate again in twos and threes.
The dominant feelings are the blue sky, and the year.
—Memories of other seasons and the billowing wind;
The light gradually altering from difficult to clear
As a page melts and a photograph develops in the backyard.
When some men came to tear down the garage across the way
The light was still clear, but the salt intoxication
Was already dissipating into the atmosphere of constant day
April brings, between the isolation and the flowers.
Now the clouds are lighter, the branches are frosted green,
And suddenly the season that had seemed so tentative before
Becomes immediate, so clear the heart breaks and the vibrant
Air is laced with crystal wires leading back from hell.
Only the distraction, and the exaggerated sense of care
Here at the heart of spring—all year long these feelings
Alternately wither and bloom, while a dense abstraction
Hides them. But now the mental dance of solitude resumes,
And life seems smaller, placed against the background
Of this story with the empty, moral quality of an expansive
Gesture made up out of trees and clouds and air.

The loneliness comes and goes, but the blue holds,
Permeating the early leaves that flutter in the sunlight

As the air dances up and down the street. Some kids yell.
A white dog rolls over on the grass and barks once. And
Although the incidents vary and the principal figures change,
Once established, the essential tone and character of a season
Stay inwardly the same day after day, like a person's.
The clouds are frantic. Shadows sweep across the lawn
And up the side of the house. A dappled sky, a mild blue
Watercolor light that floats the tense particulars away
As the distraction starts. Spring here is at first so wary,
And then so spare that even the birds act like strangers,
Trying out the strange air with a hesitant chirp or two,
And then subsiding. But the season intensifies by degrees,
Imperceptibly, while the colors deepen out of memory,
The flowers bloom and the thick leaves gleam in the sunlight
Of another city, in a past which has almost faded into heaven.
And even though memory always gives back so much more of
What was there than the mind initially thought it could hold,
Where will the separation and the ache between the isolated
Moments go when summer comes and turns this all into a garden?
Spring here is too subdued: the air is clear with anticipation,
But its real strength lies in the quiet tension of isolation
And living patiently, without atonement or regret,
In the eternity of the plain moments, the nest of care
—Until suddenly, all alone, the mind is lifted upward into
Light and air and the nothingness of the sky,
Held there in that vacant, circumstantial blue until,
In the vehemence of a landscape where the colors all disappear,
The quiet absolution of the spirit quickens into fact,
And then, into death. But the wind is cool.
The buds are starting to open on the trees.
Somewhere up in the sky an airplane drones.

THE NEAR FUTURE

FOR ROBERT DASH

I used to think that the soul
Grew by remembering, that by retaining
The character of all the times and places it had lived
And working backwards, year by year,
It reached the center of a landscape
Time couldn't penetrate, a green and white house
Surrounded by a chorus of trees,
Whose rooms were always filled with other people.
And now I think that it was just scenery,

The private illusion of a world
In which the "I" is the mind of an object,
And lacks features, and is part of the world in which it has to try to live.
For the soul knows that it's empty
And longs to dissolve, like a stray dream,
Back into nature, back into those things
Which had never seemed quite clear enough before.
But until now it could only see itself.

I used to think that there was a wall
You could touch with your hand, but not understand,
And that the soul had to pass through it alone.
I thought that other people's lives
Were like the walls of a room, keeping me inside,
Away from those things that were my real nature—

The houses, trees, and curbstones,
The noisy birds outside my bedroom window
And the thick ticking outside—
Taking the time that real things require.

Why do real things have to take so long?
I knew that time needed things, but there were so many
And they exploded like birds when I was almost close enough to touch
    them,
And then drifted back into the near future,
The center of the year.
But the furniture isn't as dense as it was
A few months ago, and it's finally quiet outside,
And there are a couple of empty rooms upstairs.

THE SUBSTITUTE FOR TIME

How things bind and blend themselves together!
—Ruskin, *Praeterita*

I came back at last to my own house.
Gradually the clear, uninhabited breath
That had sprung up where the spent soul disappeared
Curved in around me, and then it too slowly disappeared.
And I have been living here ever since
In the scope of my single mind, the confines of a heart
Which is without confinement, in a final pause
Before the threshold of the future and the warm,
Inexhaustible silence at the center of the lost world.
Now the days are sweeter than they used to be,

The memories come more quickly, and the world at twilight,
The world I live in now, is the world I dreamed about
So many years ago, and now I have.
How far it feels from that infatuation with the childish
Dream of passing through a vibrant death into my real life!
How thin time seems, how late the fragrance
Bursting from the captured moments of my childhood
Into the warm evening air that still surrounds me here.
And how the names still throb inside my mind, and how my heart
    dissolves
Into a trembling, luminous confusion of bright tears.

*

For the texture of this life is like a field of stars

In which the past is hidden in a tracery
Looming high above our lives, a tangle of bright moments
Vibrating like a cloud of fireflies in the warm summer air.
And the glow of each one is a lifetime waning,
Spending itself in the temporary consolations of a mind
Beyond any possibility of happiness, that hovers in the air
A little while and then descends into itself
And the liberation of the clear white sky inside
Where the names float like birds, and all desire dies,
And the life we longed for finds us at the end.

IN THE PARK

FOR SUSAN KOETHE

This is the life I wanted, and could never see.
For almost twenty years I thought that it was enough:
That real happiness was either unreal, or lost, or endless,
And that remembrance was as close to it as I could ever come.
And I believed that deep in the past, buried in my heart
Beyond the depth of sight, there was a kingdom of peace.
And so I never imagined that when peace would finally come
It would be on a summer evening, a few blocks away from home
In a small suburban park, with some children playing aimlessly
In an endless light, and a lake shining in the distance.

Eventually, sometime around the middle of your life,
There's a moment when the first imagination begins to wane.
The future that had always seemed so limitless dissolves,
And the dreams that used to seem so real float up and fade.
The years accumulate; but they start to take on a mild,
Human tone beyond imagination, like the sound the heart makes
Pouring into the past its hymns of adoration and regret.
And then gradually the moments quicken into life,
Vibrant with possibility, sovereign, dense, serene;
And then the park is empty and the years are still.

I think the saddest memory is of a certain kind of light,
A kind of twilight, that seemed to permeate the air

For a few years after I'd grown up and gone away from home.
It was limitless and free. And of course I was going to change,
But freedom means that only aspects ever really change,
And that as the past recedes and the future floats away
You turn into what you are. And so I stayed basically the same
As what I'd always been, while the blond light in the trees
Became part of my memory, and my voice took on the accents
Of a mind infatuated with the rhetoric of farewell.

And now that disembodied grief has gone away.
It was a flickering, literary kind of sadness,
The suspension of a life between two other lives
Of continual remembrance, between two worlds
In which there's too much solitude, too much disdain.
But the sadness that I felt was real sadness,
And this elation now a real tremor as the deepening
Shadows lengthen upon the lake. This calm is real,
But how much of the real past can it absorb?
How far into the future can this peace extend?

I love the way the light falls over the suburbs
Late on these summer evenings, as the buried minds
Stir in their graves, the hearts swell in the warm earth
And the soul settles from the air into its human home.
This is where the prodigal began, and now his day is ending
In a great dream of contentment, where all night long
The children sleep within tomorrow's peaceful arms
And the past is still, and suddenly we turn around and smile
At the memory of a vast, inchoate dream of happiness,
Now that we know that none of it is ever going to be.

Don't you remember how free the future seemed
When it was all imagination? It was a beautiful park
Where the sky was a page of water, and when we looked up,
There were our own faces, shimmering in the clear air.
And I know that this life is the only real form of happiness,
But sometimes in its midst I can hear the dense, stifled sob
Of the unreal one we might have known, and when that ends
And my eyes are filled with tears, time seems to have stopped
And we are alone in the park where it is almost twenty years ago
And the future is still an immense, open dream.

The Constructor

SUNDAY EVENING

Ideas as crystals and the logic of a violin:
The intricate evasions warming up again
For another raid on the inarticulate. And soon
The morning melody begins, the oranges and the tea,
The introspective walk about the neighborhood,
The ambient noise, the low lapping of water over stones.
The peace one finds encounters one alone,
In the memories of books, or half-remembered songs,
Or in the mild enchantments of the passive mood:
To hesitate, to brood, to linger in the library and then,
As from some green and sunny chair, arise and go.
The noons seem darker, and the adolescent
Boys that used to hang around the parking lot are gone.
More water in the eyes, more dissonant musicians in the subways,
And from the font of sense a constant, incidental drone.
It is a kind of reconfiguration, and the solitary exercise
That seeks to reaffirm its name seems hollow. The sun is lower in the sky,
And as one turns towards what had felt like home,
The windows start to flicker with a loveless flame,
As though the chambers they concealed were empty. Is this
How heaven feels? The same perspective from a different room,
Inhabiting a prospect seen from someone else's balcony
In a suspended moment—as a silver airplane silently ascends
And life, at least as one has known it, slides away?

*

I thought that people understood these things.
They show the gradual encroachment of a vast,
Impersonal system of exchanges on that innermost domain
In which each object meant another one, all singing each to each
In a beautiful regress of forgetting. Nature as a language
Faithful to its terms, yet with an almost human face
That took the dark, romantic movements of desire, love, and loss
And gave them flesh and brought them into view;
Replaced by emblems of a rarified sublime,
Like Cantor's Paradise, or Edward Witten staring into space
As the leaves fell and a little dog raced through them in the park.
Was any of that mine? Was it ever anyone's?
Time makes things seem more solid than they were,
Yet these imaginary things—the dolphins and the bells, the sunny terrace
And the bright, green wings, the distant islet on the lake—
Were never barriers, but conditions of mere being, an enchanting haze
That takes one in and like a mild surprise gives way,
As though the things that one had strained against were shards of space.
The evening air feels sweeter. The moon,
Emerging from a maze of clouds into the open sky,
Casts a thin light on the trees. Infinitely far away,
One almost seems to hear—as though the fingers of a solitary giant
Traced the pure and abstract schema of those strings
In a private movement of delight—the soundless syllables'
Ambiguous undulations, like the murmur of bees.

"I HEARD A FLY BUZZ"

FOR BRUCE AND LIVIJA RENNER

Light began to wane; it was supernaturally calm.
There was movement in the air, yet nothing moving when I looked.
I felt an inkling of the night that never came, the
Faint pre-echo of a noise I couldn't hear, or didn't want to hear—
Either from timidity, or fear, or an exaggerated sense of duty;
Or because I'd spent a lifetime trying to be good.
I thought I heard a tune from a calliope, and pieces of a
Prayer I used to say each night before I went to bed—
Now I lay me down to sleep—while a parade of images of
Neighborhoods I'd known, and friends whose humor I'd enjoyed
Meandered through my consciousness like numbers in a
Stark, mechanical affair of abstract objects in a void
—For they'd begun to feel as distant as an evening
In Balboa Park, with most of them dying, and some already dead,
Inhabiting a long, generic memory only I could read.
Life ends on a particular day, and at a particular time; and yet I thought
    that
I inhabited a world existing entirely in my head, in a constructed space
Where it was never any special time, or hot, or on a Tuesday
When the phone rang, or with the television on. I
Think that I was wrong to see my body as a kind of place
From which the soul, as entropy increases, migrates
In an upward-moving spiral of completion, a defining state
—But a subtractive one—that brings relief from hope
And freedom from complexity, escaping one by one the

Emblems of its former life and then, the waiting over,
The repentance done, ascending in a final sacrament of light into a
Vacuum filled with comprehending angels who might sing to me.
    Instead,
I found myself back home in California, sipping coffee
While an unknown insect flew, invisible, around my head.
The texture of a certain summer day came back to me,
But now in a heightened form, the simple sweetness of its presence
Mingled with the faint, metallic taste of fear, until
Each moment meant two things. The nearer I approached,
The more inscrutable it seemed. The tiny buzzing noise became an
    avalanche of
Sound whose overriding meaning was the same: *get out of here*
—Wherever "here" might be. And something spoke to me,
But when I turned around and looked I caught the image of my own
    complacency
Reflected in a mirror—a temperament defined by childish anecdotes
    and jokes
And focused on an object of dispassionate concern
Beyond itself, yet part of my experience. I finally came to see
That what I valued was a fragile and contingent life
Supported by the thought of something *opposite* that might,
At any time, break through its thin veneer. Yet all the time,
Despite that constant sense, it felt so sure, so solid.
I remember walking through a park . . .

                         And suddenly
My world felt light, then numb, and then abruptly clear.
Some faces suddenly ballooned, then blurred.
Then it got dark.

THE OTHER CONDITION

The utopia of the Other Condition gets displaced by the empirical attitude . . .
The utopia of the pure Other Condition empties or branches into God.
—Robert Musil

It eases care. And I wanted something,
But the form of my conception was so bare and
Featureless that almost nothing tangible
Could fulfill that need. It was not enough,
Though the inspiration lingered, cold and barely
Conscious of itself amid the private, pastel
Shadings and pervasive warmth, but utterly alone.
I wanted to conceive the solid song that lasts
Beyond mere memory, the vast sky entering a mind and
Gleaming there, like someone's past emerging from a
Long, involuntary dream into the unforgiving light of
Other people's feelings and the weight of the external
Obstacles that greet it, which it can't identify.
For I thought I was a stranger too, and that my real
Happiness lay somewhere in that past, beyond mere care
And reason, in the memory—or in the fantasy—of home.
How suddenly the recognitions came, and the insane
Anger that defined each moment that glared back at me,
But which has finally come to characterize my life.
What is it to be alive? And they linger in the night
Like dream words arguing their dark, unsuitable desires
That render it complete, both the concrete experiences
Sheltered in the heart, as well as those imaginary
Parts it can't possess, from that first sweet breath

Of summer to the thin, attenuated voice descanting in
An amber light, as if sheer consciousness could reach
All the way to its horizon, which is death.

It's all ambience, without any density or shape,
An intense atmosphere of grace and disappointment
With the unclarity of real life and the dead certainty
Of abstraction, like a sense of something intimate and
Strange beyond the reach of feeling. Yet out of it
The strain of day-to-day existence flows, the vagrant
Moods and platitudes that come to seem the outward form
Of one's essential being, like a gradually remembered
Melody emerging from a cave. I'd never really known
How intricate a tone of voice could be, or how evasive
The direct approach to life could finally become.
A minor shading or the faint intoxication of a word
Held in the mind—is that all sensibility can see
In its pristine innocence, and all the insubstantial,
Floating intellect that seeks to understand itself
Can understand? Nothing can bring its fragrance back
Or make it breathe again, and the traces that accumulate
As time fades mimic the appearance of unconsciousness,
Portraying it, like some primitive fabulist of the self,
Immediately, but with a miserable detachment and the
Kind of understanding that only emerges later on,
And in somebody else, and in a different form.

I have this life, and still remain dissatisfied.
Objects change, yet keep their separate trajectories,
And nothing stays. I wander through a day as someone
Else might wander quietly through my mind, and the numb
Tranquillity that covers me each night seems meaningless.

Out in the world my themes deteriorate and die.
What if these thoughts were just recalcitrant desires
Felt as despair, and all these computations of the mind
Merely sensations? The abstract darkness, death, would
Still be there and unimaginable, shadowing the years
Life wasted while the atmosphere of waiting dissipated
And the body came to realize itself, and to feel afraid.
How should one live? I kept the primitive fear at bay
By hiding it behind a screen of intimate description,
A protective diary, or concealing it inside of a serene,
Expedient creation whose insides were empty and whose
Shell was just an accidental mass of scraps and stitches,
Yet which to me has come to feel seamless and complete.
Year after year the elemental dreams keep reoccurring—
That if I could find my way to set tomorrow free again,
Or to return to sheer existence . . . Incrementally,
Like an approaching equinox, the alternating styles
Of passionate, subdued reflection, and then difference
And stillness seem to chasten and revise each other,
Until finally they realize a kind of rough equivalence.
And it seems enough. It represents a form of life
Like this one, one confined to ordinary happiness
With nothing else—nothing unasked for, unimaginable
Or unmeant—beyond its facts of consciousness and
Tense and that peculiar sense of peace that comes
As one gets older, with the waning of the fundamental
Fear of something that might be merely one's self—
As though the ache were empty and this life
Completely adequate, with rationalizing memories
And afterthoughts to render it precisely
Equal to its task, and yet not enough.

UN AUTRE MONDE

The nervous style and faintly reassuring
Tone of voice concealed inside the meanings
Incompletely grasped and constantly disappearing
As the isolated moments burst against each other
And subside—these are the aspects left behind
Once the sense is over, and the confusion spent.
They belong to the naive, perennial attempt to see
And shift the focus of experience, fundamentally
Revising what it means to feel, yet realizing
Merely some minor, disappointing alterations
In the fixed scheme of things. I bring to it
Nothing but bare need, blind, continual obsession
With the private way life passes into nothing
And a mind as fragile as a heart. It started out
Indifferently but soon became my real way of feeling,
Abstract tears, an anger retrospectively revealing
Darker interpretations of the fears that filled me to
Exploding, ill-defined desires, vague anxieties and
Satisfactions that were once so much a part of me
I miss them, and I want them back. And yet in time
They did come back as wishes, but the kind of wishes
Long ago abandoned, left behind like markers on the way
To resignation, and then as infinitely fine regrets,
And then as aspects of some near, receding world
Inert as yesterday, and no longer mine.

WHAT THE STARS MEANT

On a backwards-running clock in Lisbon,
By the marble statue of Pessoa;
On an antique astrolabe in London
Tracing out the sky above Samoa,

Thousands of miles away—in time, in place,
Each night conspires to create a myth
That stands for nothing real, yet leaves you with
The vague impression of a human face.

The fragments fly apart and shift, trembling
On the threshold of a kind of fullness:
The minor wonder of remembering;
The greater wonders of forgetfulness.

For one looks back as someone else might yearn
For a new life, and set his course upon
The polestar, bid his adieus, and move on.
The journey takes a solipsistic turn,

Forsaking starlight for an inner glow,
And reducing all human history,
All human culture—highbrow, middle, low—
To one reflecting surface, one story.

What fills the heaven of a single mind?
The things that used to fill Kant's mind with awe
—"The starry heavens and the moral law"—
Seem distant now, and difficult to find

Amid the message of satiety
Issuing from the corners of the sky,
Filled with monotonous variety:
Game shows, an interview with Princess Di,

And happy talk, and sitcoms and the news,
The shit that floats across your living room
Each weekday evening. Waiting in the pews,
Out in the desert where the cacti bloom,

Something else was forming, something stranger
Gathering in the gulf below the stairs—
As though the mystery of the manger
Were written in the day-to-day affairs

Of a world consecrated to Mammon,
Yet governed by those sacred absences
That make the spirit soar, and presences
At one remove, like the sound of Cuban

Drumbeats issuing from the Ricardos'
Love nest on the television station
Like distant thunder; or Leonardo's
"Wave that flees the site of its creation."

* * *

In the desert far beyond the city,
One hears the cadences for which one longs,
The lyrics of those half-forgotten songs
—Some of them poignant, some of them witty—

Brimming with the melody of passage;
One feels the wind that blows the soul about,
Repeating its inscrutable message;
And as night falls, one sees the stars come out.

I found myself beneath a canopy
Of scenes left out of someone else's life
—The dog that didn't bark, Rosebud, Cain's wife—
Arrayed above me in a panoply

Of glittering debris, gigantic swirls
Of stars, and slowly moving caravans
Of stars like tiny Christmas lights or pearls
Of tapioca, floating in a Danse

Macabre across the heavens as I stood,
Watching the pageant in the sky unfold.
I felt the chill of something much too old
To comprehend—not the Form of the Good,

But something inchoate and violent,
A Form of Darkness. Suddenly the songs
Floating through the revelry fell silent,
As in "The Masque of the Red Death," as throngs

Of the dead twinkled at me from above.
The intimate domain of memory
Became an endless field of entropy
Transfigured, inking in the outlines of

Eurydice entombed, Orpheus immured,
And, in the center of their universe,
That subtler diadem of stars obscured
By the brighter constellations, the Hearse.

Standing off to one side, as though bereft,
There was a figure with averted eyes,
Gesturing in a language of surprise
That took possession of my heart, yet left

The question of her meaning unresolved.
I looked at her. It was time to begin.
The apparitions in the sky dissolved,
Leaving me alone, and growing old. In

The wide, unstructured heavens overhead
The stars were still shining. When I got home,
The message light was blinking on the phone.
I don't remember what the message said.

THE CONSTRUCTOR

They strike me less as actual persons than as abstract
Ghosts of an idea: that life is the external part of
Its emotions, of the small, evaporating sentiments; but
That in isolation there might be a place where you could
Live eternally behind the high, intimidating walls of art.
They knew that in the end the parts were unimportant—that
Even as the world receded language fell away until the body
Shook with feeling and became intangible; that eventually
One's soul would be absorbed by its surroundings, breath by
Simplifying breath, advancing towards that moment when its
Work would be completed and its past restored, as though
Swept forward on a quiet, undulating wave of meaning, and
As in a trance. And so they floated through their lives,
Protected by the great, exhausted themes of the romantics:
That understanding lay in childhood; that in emancipated
Language one possessed a real way of merging opposites, of
Joining the discursive tone of reason with the weight of the
Emotions to create a finite, earthly music; that any person,
By a simple act of will, could meld the substance of his life
And the seclusion of the mind together in a single testament
Suffused with light and feeling and reverberating with the
Fundamental rhythms of the heart, and never break the spell.
But those ideas are shells now, empty as those stories of the
Soul inhabiting its lost utopia—that bright, fictitious era
When a glance could take it in, a word could start it, and
The merest touch could lead it backwards through the narrow
Ways of the imagination to a paradise of innocence and peace.

Sometimes I feel this hollow sense of satisfaction at their
Disappearance, at the loss of that seductive power to make
A world seem real and bring one's individual fantasies to
Life; but other times I feel like someone living in a fable
Of his own construction, waiting in some bleak, completely
Isolated country with no hope or history, where the minutes
Come and go and memories displace each other, leaving nothing
For the soul to do but feel them as they flow, and flow away.
I know the forms of care, and understand the grammar of desire.
I understand that life is an affair of words, and that the
Hope of duplicating it is a delusion. There is a mood that
Drains it of significance, reducing all its aspirations to
A single state of mind, and all its tenderest emotions to
An empty sense of self-importance fostered by the primitive
Confusions of some distant place and time. Is this how life
Was meant to feel? For this is how, increasingly, it does.
You *want* there to be something more than just these tedious
Realities of disillusionment and anxiousness and care, and
Then you see them rising in the distance, luminescent forms
Ascending from these categorical expressions of unmeaning
In a curve that sweeps up like the graph of an obsession.
More and more their presence comes to dominate your dreams
At night, or linger in the corner of your mind by day. You
Close your eyes and something filters into consciousness;
You try to read, but with a sense of someone watching you.
One time I'd thought they'd gone away, but gradually they
Reappeared, permeating the surrounding atmosphere with
Music swirling in and all around me like a deep refrain.
And for a while they almost seem about to welcome you, to
Show you into their imaginary garden and to tell you how

Life felt, and how the world appeared before it started:
Everything melts away, until in place of the familiar,
Inessential background you begin to see the image, slowly
Coming in and out of focus, of a face you never saw before,
As though behind this wall of words there were a solitary
Presence with an unfamiliar name and with the abstract,
Heightened features of a ghost. And then the noise stops
And the language disappears, and the semblance on the page
Stares blindly back at you until it almost starts to seem
That there might be a vision of yourself that real too—
A vision of the soul, or God, or something merely human
That could live forever with the strength of an illusion.
But when I turn away and look I see myself, by contrast,
As a purely local person, temporal, not quite complete,
Unequal to the numinous desires that brought them back to
Earth and made their world seem new again, and beautiful.
I want to feel things burst again, to read life as it was
Before its truth became apparent and its youth had faded
And the doors closed on the future. I wait here in the
Narrow dispensations of the moments, mired in a state of
Vague anticipation, working through the days as through
The pages of a schoolbook, drifting through these subtly
Recursive grammars of the heart by rote, in fragments,
As though suspended in the first, uncertain stages
Of some distant happiness; in private terms and notes
That show myself to me, but which create a personality
Half-Ariel, half-real, that lives in phrases, and whose
Animus is word association, mingling those things it
Might have been with those that one can't see or even
Consciously imagine. One gets resigned to them, but

In the way the blind become resigned to the invisible,
Or the mind to finitude. One becomes sufficient. One
Even finally attains—though only at the level of the
Personal—an empty kind of freedom, mired in disbelief,
Beset by contradictory feelings, looking back at them
Sometimes in awe, and with a sense of the impossible,
Sometimes in anger; now and then in gratitude. Yet
Now and then I find myself methodically rehearsing
One or two stock narratives, and one or two ideas,
In unadorned, discursive terms and cadences that
Seem to be inspired by the breath of God, by waves
Of silent, urgent sound proliferating through and
All around me, as the past, like some mysterious
Ventriloquist, announces them in enigmatic ways.
And then I feel a part of their confusion, and at
One with them in aspiration, sharing those desires
That fostered their illusion of a poetry of stark,
Unmediated passion that revealed the soul directly;
And their faith in its redemption through a reckless,
Youthful art, begun in gladness as a kind of refuge
From the never-ending disappointments of the ordinary,
And as solace for its fall from grace into the human.
Was that all unreal? Another obsolescent exercise in
Self-delusion, nurtured in the heart and now exhausted?
Life is what you call it, but I find no words for it
In what it has become, a language emptied of its vanity
And echoing a truer rhetoric, but a despondent one:
That the burden of a poem is to recall it to itself;
That what was said and done is all there is, and that
There are no further heavens—not even earthly ones—

Beyond the ambiguities of what actually existed; that
The notion of the soul, and reaching out in desperation
For another one, are merely versions of the beautiful;
And that the present is a prison and the past a wall.
Yet once I thought I sensed a different way of feeling,
One of bare simplicity, a respite from these solitary,
Powerful abstractions and these melodramas of the mind.
I thought I felt a moment opening like an unseen flower
Only to close again, as though something else had called it,
Or as though, beneath the disaffected surface, something
Limpid and benevolent were moving at a level of awareness
I could not yet find; and so I let the moment slide away.
One reaches back in eagerness, but in an empty exercise,
For what one might have done. One reads the histories
Of art and solitude for what they say about tomorrow,
And deciphers the illusions of the past for what they
Might illuminate about today, for they were once alive.
One tries to penetrate the different dreams of reason
Buried in their tablatures, to translate the universal
Language of their faces and the outward aspects of a
Finite, inner universe. Why is it that as one gets
Closer their incredible diversity reduces to a smooth,
Impregnable facade? Whatever else their codes might
Show or say—a mood, a moment, or a whole cosmology—
Their private meaning is a person, and it fades away
As page by page or note by note one comes to hear the
Novel's ending, not the soul that wrote it, or to hear
The music of a dead composer, not a living one; and
Then to see them as emotions that in time, or someplace
After time, might gradually give way to something real.

Why must there be so many ways to disillusionment, of
Coming to believe that no one else can feel and that
One really is alone? Sometimes I feel like nothing in
This world or any other one, now like an exile,
Now a subject of the kingdom of the inconceivable.
I wanted to look past them into what their world was
Like before they finally called it home, before there
Was a state of nature to ascend from, or a pretext for
These differences I feel. I tried to kid myself that
I could talk to them directly, mixing their traditions
With the vague one of my own to conjure the imaginary
Figure of these songs without a context; carefully
Constructing one in long, erotic sentences expressing
An unfocused state of sadness, one whose proof remained
Inviting and unknown; phrasing their encouragements
Too reasonably; fashioning their reassurances that
Someday soon my time was going to come, but meanwhile
Rearranging things to make them more believable, and
Going through the sweet, hypnotic motions of a life.
There was this chorus of strange vapors, with a name
Something like mine, and someone trying to get free.
You start to see things almost mythically, in tropes
And figurations taken from the languages of art—to
See your soul as sliding out of chaos, changeable,
Twice blessed with vagueness and a heart, the feelings
Cumbersome and unrefined, the mood a truly human one
Of absolute bewilderment; and floating up from that
To an inanimate sublime, as though some angel said
Come with me, and you woke into a featureless and
Foolish paradise your life had gradually become; or

From a dense, discordant memory into a perfect world
As empty as an afterthought, and level as a line.
One day a distant cloud appears on the horizon, and
You think your life might change. These artifacts,
Whose temper mirrors mine, still argue with the same
Impersonal intensity that nothing personal can change;
And yet one waits. Where did the stark emotions go,
Where are the flowers? Mustn't there be something to
This tenderness I feel encroaching on my mind, these
Quiet intimations of a generous, calm hour insensibly
Approaching day by day through outwardly constricted
Passages confused by light and air? It starts to seem
So effortless, and something slides away into the artless
Afterlife where dreams go, or a part that all along had
Been too close to feel begins to breathe as it becomes
Increasingly transparent, and then suddenly alive.
I think I can at last almost see through them into
Everyday unhappiness, my clear, unhampered gaze
No longer troubled by their opaque atmosphere of
Rational irrationality, their reasonable facade
An ordinary attitude, their sense of consequence
Merely illusory. Why should it matter whether
One or two of them survive? They calm the days
With undirected passion and the nights with music,
Hiding them at first, then gradually revealing them
So differently—these things I'd thought I'd never
Have—simply by vanishing together one by one, like
Breaths, like intermittent glimpses of some incomplete,
Imperfect gratitude. How could this quiet feeling
Actually exist? Why do I feel so happy?

FLEETING FORMS OF LIFE

I guess the point is that the
Task would seem that much more
Difficult without the kind of
Peace they bring me, or the

Hope I always find in their
Elaborate denials and evasions,
In these brief, extraordinary
States that settle over me.

They bring an aura of restraint,
Of things interminably delayed, of
Fantasies that organize my nights
And occupy my days with dreams.

I like to think of them as ways
To reinvent myself, as forms that
Constitute a life alternative to
Mine, but that convey a mood I

Realize can seem at times almost
Unreal, almost inhuman, almost
Willfully despondent. True,
I want to rid myself of things

That lent my life its savor,
Like those prospects of a future
That dissolved as I got older,
Or the promises of a past that

Got away somehow; but after that
I want to wake into the years and
Slowly try to re-create my world
By living in it, here and now.

AU TRAIN

I like the view. I like the clear,
Uncompromising light that seems both
Ageless and renewed year after year.
I like the way the wind dies down at
Night until the lake grows still, and
How the fog conceals it in the morning.
I like to feel the breeze come up and
Then to watch the day emerging from the
Sky's peculiar blue, with distant sounds
And subjects magnified as they approach
My mind, and it prepares to take them in.
I know that most of what there is remains
Unseen, unfelt, or subject to indifference
Or change; and yet somehow I find I want to
See things in a way that only renders them
Unreal, and finally as extensions of myself:
To look at them as aspects of my feelings,
As reflections of these transitory moods I
Know are going to fade, or dreams the years
Obliterate; and then to stare into my soul
And try to wish them back again, until they
Look essentially the same—some boats, those
Trees along the shore across the lake, that
Dense horizon line—as though refracted by my
Own imaginary memories. I look at them and
Think of how they must have looked before.
I think of all the forms of happiness, and
How I'd fantasized that it might come to me
In minor moments of transcendence when the

Earth takes on the quality of air, its light
Transformed by that intensely introspective
Gaze that finds its subject in the sky. I
Think of how my heart would start to open,
How some clouds above a tree could seem as
Close to me as leaves, while ordinary sounds
—Like birds, or distant cars—could almost
Feel as though they came from deep within me.
Where did all those feelings go? I have a
Clearer sense of my surroundings, but their
Elemental glow is gone, the mere delusion of
Deliverance seems so far away, and day-to-day
Existence is a burden, dull and full of care.
At times I think I sense it in the distance,
That unnecessary angel by whose grace the
Stones sang and my vagrant heart responded,
That conveyed my waking dreams to earth but
Left them there, confined to what they are,
Yet more than that. And then I find myself
Reflecting things, imagining a vantage point
From which the years will all seem equal, a
Conception of myself and of the world that
Locates them in retrospect and brings their
Conflict to an end. I think I might have
Seen at least some fragments of the truth
Concealed in those imaginary feelings that
Appeared to me in ways I didn't recognize,
That spoke to me in terms of consolation
And that lent me something more than words,
Yet less than wings, and that were simply
Parts of what it meant to be alive.

A PARKING LOT WITH TREES

A delusion quickly flits away; we easily contrive to make the fantasm,
as it were, hate us, because we do not understand what it essentially is.
                                                            —Robert Walser

This is a fable I conspired to believe.
Its subject is a possibility that may not be my own,
The subject of a fate that wasn't up to me,
Of things I couldn't have foreseen; and how one day I found myself
Alone, contented, more or less alive,
But only vaguely understood—a sort of life
That came to me the way the past came from confusion,
Or the plain necessities of middle age
Descended from the accidents of childhood.
Sometimes I think I'm stranded in myself
The way a character can seem suspended in a story:
As a voice, or as a witness to events—intense or boring,
Actual or unreal—it strings together
In a calm phenomenology of disappointment.
But then the landscape melts away, and the sky
Takes on the character it had when I was younger.
Where is that person who I took myself to be?
Why has my life been mostly puzzlement, and hope, and inexperience?
Its ghost is humming in the summer haze, and soon another melody
    begins,
And images of dust and sunlight float across my mind
Until I think that I can almost see myself again, this time
Impersonally—suspended in an August afternoon

That ended long ago, in thoughts that shimmered on the verge of sense
When worlds collided, or in plain, flat-footed songs
That came to me as random evocations of the past.
For I believed that none of them were accidents at all,
But aspects of a different mode of being that in time might
Yield a glimpse of something wonderful and strange;
And that behind their hidden meaning lay my life.

Sometime in 1953: a memory of a drive-in movie,
Then a view of downtown in the rain. And sometime after that
I find a memory of staring through a magnifying glass
At a dissected frog. But mostly I would dream and read
And migrate in my mind across the country while I
Fantasized about the person I intended to become.
"Life took me by the shoulders, and its wonderful gaze rested on mine."
More memories: morning fog, some pastel stucco houses
Built along a canyon, and a campfire in a desert filled with stars.
I know my dreams were no more part of me than anyone's,
And yet in retrospect I like to think that I believed they were.
I like to think that I aspired to the life I'd read about in books,
Of "yellow cocktail music," trains that took you home again and bright,
Fantastic mansions filled with rooms that led to other, brighter rooms,
That came to me like Muzak in a vast, deserted
Airport where I waited in the numb hours of the morning.
One year later I looked back at what I'd done
And found it insufficient. I remember going to a movie
Where a man kept dreaming of a clock hand slicing off his head.
I thought that there was time for me to start all over,
To embark upon a program of interior definition
That eventually might yield a quietly spectacular conclusion

(But a private one) against the gradually emerging background of late
Adolescent melodies that hadn't quite begun and
That would soon be over. Cold midwinter sunlight
Slanted through my dormitory window.
A Supreme sang *run, run, run,*
And still each year I looked and felt no older.

Sometimes a life comes true in unexpected ways.
The face that it exhibits to the world appears no different,
While its voice remains essentially the same, and inside even feels the
    same.
Time seems suspended, and the mind feels infinite again.
Meanwhile its song, like someone who has spent his day,
Meandering through a meadow, changes course with rapidly
    increasing speed
And plunges headlong down a pathway into darkness.
I came to realize that *I* was what had changed:
That even though I wanted to believe that nothing much had
    happened,
No one knew me anymore, and people I encountered seemed remote
    and strange.
I felt like an increasingly composite individual, in whose name some
Pieces of the person I had been and settings it had wanted to escape
    from
Were combined together. I thought of going back there,
Not to try to pull them back together, but to
Look at them again, because I finally wanted to include them too.
They'd disappeared; there were some highways in the valley,
And a shopping mall where children used to play.
Its features became frightening, while its tone, relaxed and

Confident at first, soon trailed nervously away
Along a meaningless digression. Like a bunch of snapshots,
Each particular seemed clear; only the whole was
Hazy with obscurity and governed by the logic of the moon.
My way of sidling into things had come and gone
And I was getting sick of what I heard: some
Half-remembered monologues whose underlying theme was always
Long, how long, delivered in the still, contorted voice of someone
Constantly alone, and which at best were fragments,
Yet which taken all together made a kind of history
In the quest tradition, one whose disconnected episodes
Receded in a narrative progression that persuaded me of things I'd
    always known.
I wanted to return to where it started: a decaying mill town
With some churches on its corners, and two statues in the square.
All night the raindrops pounded on the roof
While I prepared to try to penetrate its mysteries again
With an emotion that felt something like despair,
Yet with the hope that what had seemed too difficult last night
Might suddenly seem clearer in the morning, like a forest after rain.
I felt compelled by something that I couldn't see,
That whispered from the dark side of the mirror—by an image,
Nourished underneath a rock, of clotted viscera
And blunt, frustrated passions, that propelled me inside out
Along a road that led through danger, over cliffs and mountains
But that ended in a parking lot with trees, where people knew me
And would listen while I told them of the convoluted way
I'd come . . .
            Yet why should they believe me?
And how should I respond? I guess the fantasy took hold too soon,

Before I'd had sufficient time to think it through.
Despite the dreams, those lessons of the night that
Taught me how to live inside its complicated song it
All seems too familiar, like a script someone had written, or a reverie
    I'd planned.
I wish the songs that moved me once might come to me again
And help me understand this person that I've gradually become,
Yet long ago imagined—a perfectly ordinary one
Whose mansion is the future, but whose setting is a
Landscape of a summer afternoon, with a sky heavy in the distance
And a book resting lightly in his hands.

FROM

Falling Water

(1997)

FROM THE PORCH

The stores were bright, and not too far from home.
The school was only half a mile from downtown,
A few blocks from the Oldsmobile dealer. In the sky,
The airplanes came in low towards Lindbergh Field,
Passing overhead with a roar that shook the windows.
How inert the earth must look from far away:
The morning mail, the fantasies, the individual days
Too intimate to see, no matter how you tried;
The photos in the album of the young man leaving home.
Yet there was always time to visit them again
In a roundabout way, like the figures in the stars,
Or a life traced back to its imaginary source
In an adolescent reverie, a forgotten book—
As though one's childhood were a small midwestern town
Some forty years ago, before the elm trees died.
September was a modern classroom and the latest cars,
That made a sort of futuristic dream, circa 1955.
The earth was still uncircled. You could set your course
On the day after tomorrow. And children fell asleep
To the lullaby of people murmuring softly in the kitchen,
While a breeze rustled the pages of *Life* magazine,
And the wicker chairs stood empty on the screened-in porch.

THE CONSTANT VOICE

Above a coast that lies between two coasts
Flight 902 turns west towards San Diego.
Milwaukee falls away. The constant passenger,
Removed from character and context, resumes
His California story, gradually ascending,
Reading *Farewell, My Lovely* for the umpteenth time,
Like a book above the world, or below the noise.
I recall some houses halfway in the desert,
And how dry the trees all seemed, and temporary
Even the tallest buildings looked, with bungalows
Decaying in the Santa Ana wind. And finally
Just how small it was, and mean. Is it nostalgia
For the limited that makes the days go quickly,
Tracing out their spirals of diminishing concern?
Like all the boys who lived on Westland Avenue,
I learned to follow the trails through the canyon,
Shoot at birds with a BB gun, and dream of leaving.
What are books? To me they seemed like mirrors
Holding up a vision of the social, in which people,
Beckoning from their inaccessible preserves
Like forgotten toys, afforded glimpses of those
Evanescent worlds that certain minor writers
—Raymond Chandler say, or even Rupert Brooke—
Could visualize somehow, and bring to life again.
And though these worlds were sometimes difficult to see,
Once having seen them one returned to find the words
Still there, like a part of the surroundings

Compliant to one's will.
                              Yet these are attitudes,
And each age has its separate store of attitudes,
Its store of tropes—"In Grantchester, in Grantchester!—"
That filter through its dreams and fill its songs.
Hume tried to show that sympathy alone allows
"The happiness of strangers" to affect our lives.
Yet now and then a phrase, echoing in the mind
Long after its occasion, seems to resurrect
A world I think I recognize, and never saw.
For what was there to see? Some houses on a hill
Next to a small stream? A village filled with people
I couldn't understand? Could anyone have seen the
Transitory sweetness of the Georgians' England
And the world before the War, before *The Waste Land*?
Years are secrets, and their memories are often
Stories of a past that no one witnessed, like the
Fantasies of home one builds to rationalize
The ordinary way one's life has gone since then.
Words seem to crystallize that life in pictures—
In a postcard of a vicarage, or of a canyon
Wedged between the desert and an endless ocean—
But their clarity is fleeting. I can nearly
See the coast from here, and as I hear the engines
And the bell chimes, all those images dissolve.
And then I start to hear the murmur of that
Constant voice as distant from me as a landscape
Studied from an airplane: a contingent person
With a particular mind, and a particular will,
Descending across a desert, westward over mountains

And the sparsely peopled scrub beyond the city,
Pocked with half-filled reservoirs and rudimentary
Trails with nothing waiting for me at the end
—"And is there honey still for tea?"—
But isolated houses nestled in the hills.

SORRENTO VALLEY

On a hillside somewhere in Sorrento Valley,
My aunts and uncles sat in canvas chairs
In the blazing sun, facing a small ash tree.

There was no wind. In the distance I could see
Some modern buildings, hovering in the air
Above the wooded hillsides of Sorrento Valley.

I followed the progress of a large bumblebee
As the minister stood, offering a prayer,
Next to the young white California ash tree.

Somewhere a singer went right on repeating
When I Grow Too Old to Dream. Yet to dream *where*,
I wondered—on a hillside in Sorrento Valley,

Halfway between the mountains and the sea?
To be invisible at last, and released from care,
Beneath a stone next to a white tree?

—As though each of us were alone, and free,
And the common ground we ultimately shared
Were on a hillside somewhere in Sorrento Valley,
In the shade of a small ash tree.

SONGS MY MOTHER TAUGHT ME

There was nothing there for me to disbelieve.
—Randall Jarrell

Dvorak's "Songs My Mother Taught Me,"
From the cycle *Gypsy Melodies*, anticipates
The sonorous emotions of the Trio in F Minor,
Though without the latter's complications.
The melody is simple, while the piece's
Mood looks backwards, carried by the sweet,
Sustaining rhythms of the mother's voice
Embodied in the figure of the violin, until,
Upon the second repetition of the theme
And on a high, protracted note, it suddenly
Evaporates, while the piano lingers underneath.
The world remains indifferent to our needs,
Unchanged by what the mind, in its attempt to
Render it in terms that it can recognize,
Imagines it to be. The notes make up a story
Set entirely in the kingdom of appearance,
Filled with images of happiness and sadness
And projected on a place from which all
Evidence of what happened once has vanished—
A deserted cabin on a lake, or an isolated
Field in which two people walked together,
Or the nondescript remains of someone's home.
The place endures, unmindful and unseen,
Until its very absence comes to seem a shape

That seems to stand for something—a schematic
Face that floats above a background made of
Words that someone spoke, from which the human
Figure gradually emerges, like a shifting pattern
Drifting through a filigree of flimsy clouds
Above the massive, slowly turning globe.
Beneath the trees, beneath the constellations
Drawn from the illusions sketched by sight,
The tiny figures move in twos and threes
To their particular conclusions, like the details
Of a vision that, for all it leaves to see,
Might never have existed—its conviction spent,
Its separate shapes retracing an ascending
Curve of entropy, dissolving in that endless
Dream of physics, in which pain becomes unreal,
And happiness breaks down into its elements.

I wish there were an answer to that wish.
Why can't the unseen world—the real world—
Be like an aspect of a place that one remembers?
Why can't each thing present itself, and stay,
Without the need to be perfected or refined?
Why can't we live in some imaginary realm
Beyond belief, in which all times seem equal,
And without the space between the way things are
And how they merely seem? In which the minor,
Incidental shapes that meant the world to me
—That mean the world to me—are real too?
Suppose that time were nothing but erasure,
And that years were just whatever one had lost.

The things that managed to remain unchanged
Would seem inhuman, while the course life took
Would have a form that was too changeable to see.
The simple act of speech would make it true,
Yet at the cost of leaving nothing to believe.
Within this field, this child's imagination,
An entire universe could seem to flicker
In the span of one's attention, each succeeding
Vision mingling with the rest to form a tapestry
Containing multitudes, a wealth of incident
As various as the mind itself, yet ultimately
Composed of nothing but its mirror image:
An imaginary person, who remained, within that
Seamless web of supposition, utterly alone.

All this is preface. Last May my mother died
And I flew back to San Diego for her funeral.
Her life was uneventful, and the last ten
Years or so had seemed increasingly dependent
On a vague and doctrineless religion—a religion
Based on reassurance rather than redemption—
Filled with hopes so unspecific, and a love so
Generalized that in the end it came to seem
A long estrangement, in the course of which those
Abstract sentiments had deepened and increased,
While all the real things—the things that
Used to seem so close I couldn't see them—
Had been burnished away by distance and by time,
Replaced by hazy recollections of contentment,
And obscured beneath a layer of association

Which had rendered them, once more, invisible.
And yet the streets still looked the same to me,
And even though the incidents seemed different,
The shapes that still remained exhibited the
Reassuring patterns of a natural order—
The quiet rhythms of a world demystified,
Without those old divisions into what was real
And what was wishful thinking. In a few days
Everything had altered, and yet nothing changed—
That was the anomalous event that happened
In the ordinary course of things, from which the
Rest of us were simply absent, or preoccupied,
Or busy with arrangements for the flowers,
The music, the reception at the house for various
Cousins, aunts, and uncles and, from next door,
Mr. Palistini with his tooth of gold. At
Length the house was empty, and I went outside.
It struck me that this place, which overnight
Had almost come to seem a part of me, was actually
The same one I had longed for years to leave.
There were differences of course—another
House or two, and different cars—and yet what
Startled me was how familiar it all seemed—
The numbers stenciled on the curb, the soap-dish
In the bathroom, the boxes still in the garage—
As though the intricate evasions of the years
Had left their underlying forms unchanged.
And this is not to say those fables were untrue,
But merely that their spells were incomplete—
Incomplete and passing. For although we can't

Exist without our fantasies, at times they
Start to come apart like clouds, to leave us
Momentarily alone, within an ordinary setting—
Disenchanted and alone, but also strangely free,
And suddenly relieved to find a vast, inhuman
World, completely independent of our lives
And yet behind them all, still there.

THE SECRET AMPLITUDE

I

Perhaps the hardest feeling is the one
Of unrealized possibility:
Thoughts left unspoken, actions left undone

That seemed to be of little consequence
To things considered in totality;
And yet that might have made a difference.

Sometimes the thought of what one might have done
Starts to exhaust the life that it explains,
After so much of what one knew has gone.

I guess that all things happen for the best,
And that whatever life results remains,
In its own fashion, singularly blest.

Yet when I try to think about the ways
That brought me here, I think about places
Visited, about particular days

Whiled away with a small handful of friends,
Some of them gone; and about the traces
Of a particular movement, that ends

In mild effects, but that originates
In the sheer "wonder of disappointment,"
Ascending in an arc that resonates

Through the heavens, before a dying fall.
I don't know what Wittgenstein might have meant
By *nothing is hidden*, if not that all

The aspects of one's life are there to see.
But last month, coming back on the Metro
From the Basilica of Saint-Denis,

My sense of here and now began to melt
Into a sensation of vertigo
I realized that I had never felt.

II

Start with the condition of the given:
A room, a backyard, or a city street.
Next, construct an idea of heaven

By eliminating the contingent
Accidents that make it seem familiar.
Spanning these polarities—the stringent

Vacuum and the sound of a lawn mower—
Find the everyday experiences
Making up our lives, set on the lower

Branches of the tree of knowledge. Is *this*
What people mean by living in the world?
A region of imaginary bliss,

Uncontaminated by reflection,
Rationalized by the controlling thought
Of simple beauty, of the perfection

Of the commonplace through acquiescence?
Think of a deeper order of beauty,
A kind of magnificence whose essence

Lies in estrangement, the anxiety
Of the unrecognized, in resistance,
And in the refusal of piety.

Nothing comes of nothing: what ideals
Alter is the look of things, the changing
Surfaces their argument reveals

To be illusory. Yet one still tries,
Pulled inward by the promissory thought
Of something time can never realize,

Both inexhaustible and self-contained;
Of something waiting to be discovered
In the dominion of the unattained.

III

I always think about it in a way
So inflected by the thought of places,
And of my distance from them; by other

People, and the measure of another
Year since they departed, that they get hard
To separate, like the thought of a day

From the day itself. I suppose the proof,
If there is one, is by analogy
With the kind of adolescent "knowledge"

I had on those afternoons in college
When I'd go to New York, and the evening
Deepened, and then the lights came on. Aloof,

Yet somehow grounded in the real, it's
Like an abstract diagram of a face,
Or the experience of memory

Drained of its vivifying imagery
—Of Geoff's cigars, for instance, or Willy's
Collision with the pillar at the Ritz—

Until the pure experience remains.
For over time, the personal details
Came to mean less to me than the feeling

Of simply having lived them, revealing
Another way of being in the world,
With all the inwardness it still sustains,

And the promise of happiness it brought.
So it began to take over my life—
Not like some completely arbitrary

Conception someone had imposed on me,
But more and more like a second nature;
Until it became my abiding thought.

IV

How much can someone actually retain
Of a first idea? What the day was,
Or what the flowers in the room were like,

Or how the curtains lifted in the breeze?
The meaning lies in what a person does
In the aftermath of that abundance,

On an ordinary day in August
In the still air, beneath a milk-white sky—
As something quickens in the inner room

No one inhabits, filling its domain
With the sound of an ambiguous sigh
Muffled by traffic noises. Underneath,

The movement starts to recapitulate
Another season and another life,
Walking through the streets of Barcelona,

Its alleys and its accidents combined
Into an arabesque of feeling, rife
With imprecision, blending everything

Into a song intended to obscure,
Like the song of the wind, and so begin
To repeat the fallacy of the past:

That it was pure, and that the consummate
Achievement is to bring it back again.
Would it make any difference? Each breath

Anticipates the next, until the end.
Nothing lasts. The imperative of change
Is what the wind repeats, and night brings dreams

Illuminating the transforming thought
Of the familiar context rendered strange,
The displacement of the ordinary.

V

I hadn't been to Paris in six years.
My hotel room was like a pleasant cell.
On the plane I'd been bothered by vague fears

Of being by myself for the first time,
Or recognizing the sound of the bell
Of St-Germain-des-Prés, or a street mime

At Deux Magots, and being overwhelmed
By the sensation of being alone.
Even with a friend, from the distant realm

108

Of Rome, I couldn't shake the impression
Of exile, as though I'd come to atone
For some indescribable transgression—

A state of anonymity, without
Anonymity's deep sense of pardon.
We ate, and walked about, and talked about

The true nature of the sentimental.
Later, as I imagined the garden
Of the new Bibliothèque Nationale

Drowsing in its shade of information,
I felt the peace of insignificance,
Of a solitude like a vocation

To be inhabited, to be explored
With the single-minded perseverance
Of a blind man whose sight had been restored.

Everything seemed so mindless and abstract,
Stripped of the personality I knew.
The evening was like a secret compact,

And though it was May, the night air felt cold.
The sky was black. The sky was gold and blue
Above an Eiffel Tower lit with gold.

VI

What is the abstract, the impersonal?
Are they the same? And whence this grandiose
Geography of a few emotions?

Think of an uninhabited landscape,
With its majesty rendered otiose
By a stranger's poverty of feeling;

Then contemplate that state without a name
In which something formless and inchoate
Stirs in an act of definition, like

A thought becoming conscious of itself,
For which the words are always late, too late.
The motion spreads its shape across the sky,

Unburdened by causality and death.
Where is that paradise? Where is that womb
Of the unreal, that expansiveness

That turned the mountains into vacant air,
The empty desert to an empty tomb
On Sunday, with the body set aside,

The sense of diminution giving way,
Through the oscillations of the sublime,
To an infinite expanse of spirit?

If only one could know, at this remove,
The private alchemy, obscured by time,
By which an inhospitable terrain

Became an open space, "a fresh, green breast"
Of a new world of such magnificence
That those who entered were as though reborn,

And everything they heard and saw and felt
Melted into shape and significance;
And what that secret amplitude was like.

VII

But is there even anything to know?
Linger over the cases: the dead friends,
And what the obituaries omit

And one can only imagine: what it
Must have felt like at the end, suspended
Between two impossible tasks, as though

The burden of each day were to rebut
A presumption of disillusionment
And a sense of hopelessness, deflected

By the daily routine, yet protected
By the cave of the imagination;
Until at last the inner door slammed shut.

When did it all become unbearable?
The question begs the questions of their lives
Asked from the inside, taking for granted

Their very being, as though enchanted
By the way the settings, in retrospect,
Make up the logic of a parable

Whose incidents make no sense, and by how
Time tries to project a kind of order,
And the terrifying clarity it brings,

Into the enigma of the last things—
A vodka bottle lying on the floor,
An offhand remark ("I'll be going now")—

With everything contained, as in a proof,
In a few emblems of finality:
The bullet in the mouth. The sharp report

That no one else can hear. The sharp report
That only someone else *could* hear. The long,
Irrevocable transport from the roof.

VIII

If God in Heaven were a pair of eyes
Whose gaze could penetrate the camouflage
Of speech and thought, the innocent disguise

Of a person looking in the mirror;
If a distant mind, in its omniscience,
Could reflect and comprehend the terror

Obscured by the trappings of the body—
If these possibilities were real,
Everything would look the same: a cloudy

Sky low in the distance, and a dead tree
Visible through the window. The same thoughts
Would engage the mind: that one remains free

In a limited sense, and that the rough
Approximation of eternity
Contained in every moment is enough.

What sponsors the idea of a god
Magnificent in its indifference,
And inert above the shabby, slipshod

Furnishings that constitute the human?
What engenders the notion of a state
Transcending the familiar, common

Ground on which two people walked together
Some twenty years ago, through a small park?
The benches remain empty. The weather

Changes with the seasons, which feel the same.
The questions trace out the trajectory
Of a person traveling backwards, whose name

Occupies a space between death and birth;
Of someone awkwardly celebrating
A few diminished angels, and the earth.

IX

It's been nine years since the telephone call
From Mark, and a year since the one from John.
And it's as though nothing's *changed*, but that all

The revisions were finally over.
And yet now more than half my life is gone,
Like those years of waiting to discover

That hidden paradise of the recluse
I was always just about to enter—
Until it came to seem like an excuse

For the evasion of intimacy.
At Willy's memorial last winter,
Edward Albee spoke of his privacy,

And how at last he wandered up the stairs
To a "final privacy." And perhaps
The illusions that keep us from our cares

Are projections of our mortality,
Of the impulse inside the fear it maps
Onto the sky, while in reality

The fear continues underneath. I guess
That despite the moments of resplendence
Like the one in Paris, it's still the less

Insistent ones that come to rest within.
I don't know why the thought of transcendence
Beckons us, or why we strive for it in

Solitary gestures of defiance,
Or try to discover it in our dreams,
Or by rending the veil of appearance.

Why does it have to issue from afar?
Why can't we find it in the way life *seems*?
As Willy would have said—*So, here we are.*

A PATHETIC LANDSCAPE

The purpose remains constant: to change a
Pretense of description into one of feeling,
And to translate the face of the external world
Into a language spoken in the mind, and with

The inward eye survey the frozen aspects of a
Wilderness illuminated by a cold, imaginary sun.
Somehow these artifacts, which come to next to
Nothing on their own, collectively define a

Discourse of the individual, vibrating with a
Solipsistic rhetoric sustained by a succession of
Minute, spectacular effects, and even superficially
Alive; yet finally incomplete, its terms confined

To this austere, conversational vernacular. What
Is plain language anyway? Is it the one you think,
Or hear, or one that you imagine? Can it incorporate
The numinous as well as the particular, and the ways

Ideas move, and the aftertaste that a conviction leaves
Once its strength has faded? I don't believe it anymore,
But I can hear it sighing in the wind, and feel it in the
Movement of the leaves outside my window as the season

Deepens into ice and silence. It speaks too slowly,
While the sentiments it once could bring to life feel
Dissipated now, the blood runs colder in the veins,
This room in which I live seems smaller every day

And every time I hear those tones of voice that
Used to mean the world to me, and which will not
Come back to me again, even the wind turns bitter
And the clouds stream furiously across the sun.

MORNING IN AMERICA

It gradually became a different country
After the reversal, dominated by a distant,
Universal voice whose favorite word was *never*,
Changing its air of quiet progress into one of
Rapidly collapsing possibilities, and making me,
Even here at home, a stranger. I felt its tones
Engaging me without expression, leaving me alone
And waiting in the vacuum of its public half-life,
Quietly confessing my emotions, taking in its cold
Midwinter atmosphere of violence and muted rage. I
Wanted to appropriate that anger, to convey it, not
In a declamatory mode, but in some vague and private
Language holding out, against the clear, inexorable
Disintegration of a nation, the claims of a renewed
Internal life, in these bleak months of the new year.
That was my way of ruling out everything discordant,
Everything dead, cruel, or soulless—by assiduously
Imagining the pages of some legendary volume marked
Forever, but without ever getting any closer. As I
Got older it began to seem more and more hopeless,
More and more detached—until it only spoke to me
Impersonally, like someone gradually retreating,
Not so much from his life as from its settings,
From the country he inhabits; as the darkness
Deepens in the weeks after the solstice.

HENRIETTA

In some small town, one indifferent summer.
—John Ashbery

The limitless blue sky is still a page
Beyond imagination. The incidental
Clouds traverse it as they did in 1933,
Or above Pearl Harbor, or above the
Outskirts of a prosperous North Texas town
When both of my grandparents were young.
April frosts the trees with green,
The flowers start to blossom in the shade,
And as the seasons come around again
The unsung melody resumes above the leaves—
Emotionless and free, its character unmarked by time,
As though a century had opened just an hour ago.
The terms our lives propose elude them,
And the underlying themes that bind them into wholes
Are difficult to hear inside an isolated room—
Receding, like the memory of a particular afternoon
That flickers like a smile across the quiet face of time,
Into a private history. And my father's parents
Stumble through the Crash into an unfamiliar world
With no relation to the one they'd had in mind—
As in certain parlor games, or manipulated photographs,
In which the intricate details of individual lives
Dissolve into the accidental shapes that they compose.
Sometimes the ordinary light stops shining,

And the sky above the bungalows takes on the dull,
Metallic sheen of some premonitory gong
Suspended high above our cares, above our lives.
The grand piano in the living room,
The antimacassars on the damasked chairs—
Sometimes their distant counterpoint returns,
As though diurnal time had halted, and the street
Were like a boulevard illuminated by the moon
Or bathed in the dim aquarium light of an eclipse.
The birds know it, and from deep inside
The rooms seem lit with echoes of the faint,
Unearthly music that from time to time one hears
Beneath the incidental music of the human—
The disenchanting music of indifference;
Of the dark, indifferent spheres.

When I was seven or eight my father
Drove us all halfway across the country
In an emerald Chevrolet with benchlike seats
To visit my grandparents in Texas.
The coastal vegetation gradually gave way
To an interminable, scrub-filled desert,
Rhyming lines of signs for Burma-Shave,
And railroad tracks with wooden water towers.
The house was cavernous and cool and clean,
With a pecan tree in the backyard, and flowers
Set along the side that faced a rudimentary swing.
Lincrusta-Walton walls, the tubular brass bed
Where my grandfather kept snoring as I tried to sleep—
For all that I can see, these things weren't real,

And yet their vestiges have managed to survive
As on a hidden stream, and with a logic of their own,
Like minor histories made up from vagrant
Images that seem to roam at random in your mind,
Or thoughts your memory carries on its light,
Rejuvenating breeze, that brings them back to life
With an intensity they never had in life—
The images of Nana's hair and Bobby's glasses
Floating in an atmosphere of fading mental
Snapshots of a miniature downtown, and rows of
Dark cars parked diagonally by the sidewalks,
And the barber shop he opened after the bank collapsed.
After my grandmother died, he stayed on for a while
In their unlocked house, amid her "lovely things"
—The candlesticks, the sparkling cut-crystal bowls—
That strangers wandered in and stole. When
We returned, he'd moved into a little bungalow
Next to some open fields, which he and I methodically
Patrolled on Sundays in his dull black Ford,
Shooting birds and rabbits with a .410 shotgun.
He died my freshman year in college.
Last week, when I was back in California,
My father talked about the pleasure he'd derived
From his collection of fine guns, which were
Among the few things that he'd taken when he moved,
And which, while he lay dying in the hospital
During his final illness, were stolen too.

A writer's secret is an uncorrupted world.
Nobody lives there, and the intricate affairs

Of state, or those of day to day existence
Wait undreamed of; while their echoes
Slide into a residue of multiple erasures.
Reading all this over, I have the sense
That what I've just described was just a pretext,
And that what I really meant was something
Utterly removed from Henrietta and the little
Stories I remember. Like an unmarked page,
One's universe extends beyond its comprehending mind,
And what had seemed so momentarily clear
In its eternal instant, flickers into obscurity
Along the dull, unwritten passages of time.
The penitent rests his case. My father
Finished college, left home for a conservatory,
And played with orchestras in Europe and New York
Until the war came and he joined the navy.
What are years? Their shapes accelerate and blur
Into an outline of my life, into this specious
Present I can find no words for, whose
Extent is recollection and the patterns that it
Throws upon the firmament of widely scattered stars,
On the inscrutable dark matter at its core.
The soul invents a story of its passing,
Yet the fables it creates, like chamber music,
Float through half-remembered rooms, where someone
Waits at a piano, or some open fields in Texas,
Where a train rolls by and clouds drift slowly overhead.
I said I thought the real song lay deeper,
Yet its words are snatches of those adolescent times
That wax and wane at random, as one lies in bed

Before the healing wave of sleep; or while one lingers
Outside on a summer evening, with a dazzling canopy of stars
Surrounding a mind like a jar full of fireflies.
The metaphors that amplify the one we call the world
Are surface eddies, while the underlying stream
Endures below the frequency of consciousness,
Like the inaudible sensation of a buried organ note
That seems to issue from within. The rest
Is merely speculation, fading from one's attention
Like the diary of a dream recorded years and years ago,
And apprehended from the vantage point of age
—And the only real vantage point is age—
That seems at first too close, and then too clear,
But ultimately of no real concern at all.
I guess what finally keeps the time are just these
Chronicles of the smaller worlds—the private
Journals, the chronologies that span the century,
While something lurks beyond their borders,
Beyond our power to imagine: an elementary state
Unshaped by feeling, uncorrupted by experience
And converging on an old, impersonal ideal
Bereft of human features, whose enigmatic face
Still broods behind the sky above the town—
Inert and beautiful, but with the permanence of an idea
Too remote from us, and too tangible to retrieve.

FALLING WATER

I drove to Oak Park, took two tours,
And looked at some of the houses.
I took the long way back along the lake.
The place that I came home to—a cavernous
Apartment on the East Side of Milwaukee—
Seems basically a part of that tradition,
With the same admixture of expansion and restraint:
The space takes off, yet leaves behind a nagging
Feeling of confinement, with the disconcerting sense
That while the superficial conflicts got resolved,
The underlying tensions brought to equilibrium,
It isn't yet a place in which I feel that I can live.
Imagine someone reading. Contemplate a man
Oblivious to his settings, and then a distant person
Standing in an ordinary room, hemmed in by limitations,
Yet possessed by the illusion of an individual life
That blooms within its own mysterious enclosure,
In a solitary space in which the soul can breathe
And where the heart can stay—not by discovering it,
But by creating it, by giving it a self-sustaining
Atmosphere of depth, both in the architecture,
And in the unconstructed life that it contains.
In a late and very brief remark, Freud speculates
That space is the projection of a "psychic apparatus"
Which remains almost entirely oblivious to itself;
And Wright extols "that primitive sense of shelter"
Which can turn a house into a refuge from despair.

I wish that time could bring the future back again
And let me see things as they used to seem to me
Before I found myself alone, in an emancipated state—
Alone and free and filled with cares about tomorrow.
There used to be a logic in the way time passed
That made it flow directly towards an underlying space
Where all the minor, individual lives converged.
The moments borrowed their perceptions from the past
And bathed the future in a soft, familiar light
I remembered from home, and which has faded.
And the voices get supplanted by the rain,
The nights seem colder, and the angel in the mind
That used to sing to me beneath the wide suburban sky
Turns into dreamwork and dissolves into the air,
While in its place a kind of monument appears,
Magnificent in isolation, compromised by proximity
And standing in a small and singular expanse—
As though the years had been a pretext for reflection,
And my life had a been phase of disenchantment—
As the faces that I cherished gradually withdraw,
The reassuring settings slowly melt away,
And what remains is just a sense of getting older.
In a variation of the parable, the pure of heart
Descend into a kingdom that they never wanted
And refused to see. The homely notions of the good,
The quaint ideas of perfection swept away like
Adolescent fictions as the real forms of life
Deteriorate with manically increasing speed,
The kind man wakes into a quiet dream of shelter,
And the serenity it brings—not in reflection,

But in the paralyzing fear of being mistaken,
Of losing everything, of acquiescing in the
Obvious approach (the house shaped like a box;
The life that can't accommodate another's)—
As the heart shrinks down to tiny, local things.

Why can't the more expansive ecstasies come true?
I met you more than thirty years ago, in 1958,
In Mrs. Wolford's eighth-grade history class.
All moments weigh the same, and matter equally;
Yet those that time brings back create the fables
Of a happy or unsatisfying life, of minutes
Passing on the way to either peace or disappointment—
Like a paper calendar on which it's always autumn
And we're back in school again; or a hazy afternoon
Near the beginning of October, with the World Series
Playing quietly on the radio, and the windows open,
And the California sunlight filling up the room.
When I survey the mural stretched across the years
—Across my heart—I notice mostly small, neglected
Parts of no importance to the whole design, but which,
In their obscurity, seem more permanent and real.
I see the desks and auditorium, suffused with
Yellow light connoting earnestness and hope that
Still remains there, in a space pervaded by a
Soft and supple ache too deep to contemplate—
As though the future weren't real, and the present
Were amorphous, with nothing to hold on to,
And the past were there forever. And the art
That time inflicts upon its subjects can't

Eradicate the lines sketched out in childhood,
Which harden into shapes as it recedes.
I wish I knew a way of looking at the world
That didn't find it wanting, or of looking at my
Life that didn't always see a half-completed
Structure made of years and filled with images
And gestures emblematic of the past, like Gatsby's
Light, or Proust's imbalance on the stones.
I wish there were a place where I could stay
And leave the world alone—an enormous stadium
Where I could wander back and forth across a field
Replete with all the incidents and small details
That gave the days their textures, that bound the
Minutes into something solid, and that linked them
All together in a way that used to seem eternal.
We used to go to dances in my family's ancient
Cadillac, which blew up late one summer evening
Climbing up the hill outside Del Mar. And later
I can see us steaming off the cover of the Beatles'
Baby-butcher album at your house in Mission Bay;
And three years later listening to the Velvet
Underground performing in a roller skating rink.
Years aren't texts, or anything *like* texts;
And yet I often think of 1968 that way, as though
That single year contained the rhythms of the rest,
As what began in hope and eagerness concluded in
Intractable confusion, as the wedding turned into a
Puzzling fiasco over poor John Godfrey's hair.
The parts were real, and yet the dense and living
Whole they once composed seems broken now, its

Voice reduced to disembodied terms that speak to me
More distantly each day, until the tangled years
Are finally drained of feeling, and collapse into a
Sequence of the places where we lived: your parents'
House in Kensington, and mine above the canyon;
Then the flat by Sears in Cambridge, where we
Moved when we got married, and the third floor
Of the house on Francis Avenue, near Harvard Square;
The big apartment in Milwaukee where we lived the
Year that John was born, and last of all the
House in Whitefish Bay, where you live now
And all those years came inexplicably undone
In mid-July. The sequence ended late last year.
Suppose we use a lifetime as a measure of the world
As it exists for one. Then half of mine has ended,
While the fragment which has recently come to be
Contains no vantage point from which to see it whole.
I think that people are the sum of their illusions,
That the cares that make them difficult to see
Are eased by distance, with their errors blending
In an intricate harmony, their truths abiding
In a subtle "spark" or psyche (each incomparable,
Yet each the same as all the others) and their
Disparate careers all joined together in a tangled
Moral vision whose intense, meandering design
Seems lightened by a pure simplicity of feeling,
As in grief, or in the pathos of a life
Cut off by loneliness, indifference or hate,
Because the most important thing is human happiness—
Not in the sense of private satisfactions, but of

Lives that realize themselves in ordinary terms
And with the quiet inconsistencies that make them real.
The whole transcends its tensions, like the intimate
Reflections on the day that came at evening, whose
Significance was usually overlooked, or misunderstood,
Because the facts were almost always unexceptional.
Two years ago we took our son to Paris. Last night
I picked him up and took him to a Lou Reed show,
And then took him home. I look at all the houses as I
Walk down Hackett Avenue to work. I teach my classes,
Visit friends, cook introspective meals for myself,
Yet in the end the minutes don't add up. What's lost
Is the perception of the world as something good
And held in common; as a place to be perfected
In the kinds of everyday divisions and encounters
That endowed it with integrity and structure,
And that merged its private moments with the past.
What broke it into pieces? What transformed the
Flaws that gave it feeling into objects of a deep and
Smoldering resentment—like coming home too early,
Or walking too far ahead of you on the rue Jacob?
I wish that life could be a window on the sun,
Instead of just this porch where I can stand and
Contemplate the wires that lace the parking lot
And feel it moving towards some unknown resolution.
The Guggenheim Museum just reopened. Tonight I
Watched a segment of the news on PBS—narrated by a
Woman we met years ago at Bob's—that showed how
Most of Wright's interior had been restored,
And how the ramp ascends in spirals towards the sky.

I like the houses better—they flow in all directions,
Merging with the scenery and embodying a milder,
More domestic notion of perfection, on a human scale
That doesn't overwhelm the life that it encloses.
Isn't there a way to feel at home within the
Confines of this bland, accommodating structure
Made of souvenirs and emblems, like the hammock
Hanging in the backyard of an undistinguished
Prairie School house in Whitefish Bay—the lineal,
Reduced descendent of the "Flameproof" Wright house
Just a block or two away from where I live now?
I usually walk along that street on Sunday,
Musing on how beautiful it seems, how aspects of it
Recapitulate the Oak Park house and studio, with
Open spaces buried in a labyrinthine interior,
And with the entrance half concealed on the side—
A characteristic feature of his plans that made it
Difficult to find, although the hope was that in
Trying to get inside, the visitor's eye would come to
Linger over subtleties he might have failed to see—
In much the way that in the course of getting older,
And trying to reconstruct the paths that led me here,
I found myself pulled backwards through these old,
Uncertain passages, distracted by the details,
And meeting only barriers to understanding why the
Years unfolded as they did, and why my life
Turned out the way it has—like his signature
"Pathway of Discovery," with each diversion
Adding to the integrity of the whole.

*

There is this *sweep* life has that makes the
Accidents of time and place seem small.
Everything alters, and the personal concerns
That love could hold together for a little while
Decay, and then the world seems strange again,
And meaningless and free. I miss the primitive
Confusions, and the secret way things came to me
Each evening, and the pain. I still wonder
Where the tears went, standing in my room each day
And quietly inhabiting a calm, suspended state
Enveloped by the emptiness that scares and thrills me,
With the background noise cascading out of nothing
Like a song that makes the days go by, a song
Incorporating everything—not into what it says,
But simply in the way it touches me, a single
Image of dispersal, the inexhaustible perception
Of contingency and transience and isolation.
It brings them back to me. I have the inwardness
I think I must have wanted, and the quietude,
The solitary temper, and this space where I can
Linger with the silence curling all around me
Like the sound of pure passage, waiting here
Surrounded by the furniture, the books and lists
And all these other emblems of the floating world,
The prints of raindrops that begin as mist, that fall
Discreetly through the atmosphere, and disappear.
And then I feel them in the air, in a reserved,
More earthly music filled with voices reassembling
In a wellspring of remembrance, talking to me again,
And finding shelter in the same evasive movements

I can feel in my own life, cloaked in a quiet
Dignity that keeps away the dread of getting old,
And fading out of other people's consciousness,
And dying—with its deepest insecurities and fears
Concealed by their own protective colorations,
As the mind secretes its shell and calls it home.
It has the texture of an uncreated substance,
Hovering between the settings it had come to love
And some unformulated state I can't imagine—
Waiting for the telephone to ring, obsessed with
Ways to occupy these wide, unstructured hours,
And playing records by myself, and waking up alone.
All things are disparate, yet subject to the same
Intense, eradicating wills of time and personality,
Like waves demolishing the walls love seemed to build
Between our lives and emptiness, the certainty they
Seemed to have just two or three short years ago,
Before the anger spread its poison over everything.
I think about the way our visions locked together
In a nightmare play of nervousness and language,
Living day to day inside the concentrated
Force of that relentless argument, whose words
Swept over us in formless torrents of anxiety, two
People clinging to their versions of their lives
Almost like children—living out each other's
Intermittent fantasies, that fed upon themselves
As though infected by some vile, concentrated hatred,
Who then woke up and planned that evening's dinner.
It's all memories now, and distance. Miles away
The cat is sleeping on the driveway, John's in school,

And sunlight filters through a curtain in the kitchen.
Nothing really changes—the external world intrudes
And then withdraws, and then becomes continuous again.
I went downtown today and got a lamp with pendant
Lanterns made of opalescent art glass—part, I guess,
Of what this morning's paper called the "Wright craze."
I like the easy way the days go by, the parts of aging
That have come to seem familiar, and the uneventful
Calm that seems to settle on the house at night.
Each morning brings the mirror's reassuring face,
As though the years had left the same enduring person
Simplified and changed—no longer vaguely desperate,
No longer torn, yet still impatient with himself
And still restless; but drained of intricacy and rage,
Like a mild paradox—uninteresting in its own right,
Yet existing for the sake of something stranger.
Now and then our life comes over me, in brief,
Involuntary glimpses of that world that blossom
Unexpectedly, in fleeting moments of regret
That come before the ache, the pang that gathers
Sharply, like an indrawn breath—a strange and
Thoughtful kind of pain, as though a steel
Band had somehow snapped inside my heart.
I don't know. But what I do know is that
None of it is ever going to come to me again.
Why did I think a person only distantly like me
Might finally represent my life? What aspects
Of my attitudes, my cast of mind, my inconclusive
Way of tossing questions at the world had I
Supposed might realize another person's fantasies

And turn her into someone else—who gradually became
A separate part of me, and argued with the very
Words I would have used, and looked at me through
Eyes I'd looked at as though gazing at myself?
I guess we only realize ourselves in dreams,
Or in these self-reflexive reveries sustaining
All the charms that contemplation holds—until the
Long enchantment of the soul with what it sees
Is lifted, and it startles at a space alight with
Objects of its infantile gaze, like people in a mall.
I saw her just the other day. I felt a kind of
Comfort at her face, one tinctured with bemusement
At the strange and guarded person she'd become—
Attractive, vaguely friendly, brisk (*too* brisk),
But no one I could think might represent my life.
Why did I even try to see myself in what's outside?
The strangeness pushes it away, propels the vision
Back upon itself, into these regions filled with
Shapes that I can wander through and never see,
As though their image were inherently unreal.
The houses on a street, the quiet backyard shade,
The rooms restored to life with bric-a-brac—
I started by revisiting these things, then slowly
Reconceiving them as forms of loss made visible
That balanced sympathy and space inside an
Abstract edifice combining reaches of the past
With all these speculations, all this artful
Preening of the heart. I sit here at my desk,
Perplexed and puzzled, teasing out a tangled
Skein of years we wove together, and trying to

Combine the fragments of those years into a poem.
Who cares if life—if someone's actual life—is
Finally insignificant and small? There's still a
Splendor in the way it flowers once and fades
And leaves a carapace behind. There isn't time to
Linger over why it happened, or attempt to make its
Mystery come to life again and last, like someone
Still embracing the confused perceptions of himself
Embedded in the past, as though eternity lay there—
For heaven's a delusion, and eternity is in the details,
And this tiny, insubstantial life is all there is—
And that would be enough, but for the reoccurring
Dreams I often have of you. Sometimes at night
The banished unrealities return, as though a room
Suffused with light and poetry took shape around me.
Pictures line the walls. It's early summer.
Somewhere in *Remembrance of Things Past*, Marcel,
Reflecting on his years with "Albertine"—with X—
Suggests that love is just a consciousness of distance,
Of the separation of two lives in time and space.
I think the same estrangement's mirrored in each life,
In how it seems both adequate and incomplete—part
Day to day existence, part imaginary construct
Beckoning at night, and sighing through my dreams
Like some disconsolate chimera, or the subject
Of a lonely, terrifying sadness; or the isolation
Of a quiet winter evening, when the house feels empty,
And silence intervenes. But in the wonderful
Enclosure opening in my heart, I seem to recognize
Our voices lilting in the yard, inflected by the

Rhythms of a song whose words are seamless
And whose lines are never ending. I can almost
See the contours of your face, and sense the
Presence of the trees, and reimagine all of us
Together in a deep, abiding happiness, as if the
Three of us inhabited a fragile, made-up world
That seemed to be so permanent, so real.
I have this fantasy: It's early in the evening.
You and I are sitting in the backyard, talking.
Friends arrive, then drinks and dinner, conversation . . .

The lovely summer twilight lasts forever . . .

                                              What's the use?
What purpose do these speculations serve? What
Mild enchantments do these meditations leave?
They're just the murmurs of an age, of middle age,
That help to pass the time that they retrieve
Before subsiding, leaving everything unchanged.
Each of us at times has felt the future fade,
Or seen the compass of his life diminished,
Or realized some tangible illusion was unreal.
Driving down to Evanston last week, I suddenly
Remembered driving down that road eight years ago,
So caught up in some story I'd just finished
That I'd missed the way the countryside was changing—
How in place of trees there now were office towers
And theme parks, parts of a confusing panoply of
Barns and discount malls transfiguring a landscape
Filled with high, receding clouds, and rows of flimsy

Houses in what used to be a field. I thought of
Other people's lives, and how impossible it seemed
To grasp them on the model of my own—as little
Mirrors of infinity—or sense their forms of
Happiness, or in their minor personal upheavals
Feel the sweep of time reduced to human scale
And see its abstract argument made visible.
I thought of overarching dreams of plenitude—
How life lacks shape until it's given one by love,
And how each soul is both a kingdom in itself
And part of some incorporating whole that
Feels and has a face and lets it live forever.
All of these seemed true, and cancelled one another,
Leaving just the feeling of an unseen presence
Tracing out the contours of a world erased,
Like music tracing out the contours of the mind—
For life has the form of a winding curve in space
And in its wake the human figure disappears.
Look at our surroundings—where a previous age
Could visualize a landscape we see borders,
Yet I think the underlying vision is the same:
A person positing a world that he can see
And can't contain, and vexed by other people.
Everything is possible; some of it seemed real
Or nearly real, yet in the end it spoke to me alone,
In phrases echoing the isolation of a meager
Ledge above a waterfall, or rolling across a vast,
Expanding plain on which there's always room,
But only room for one. It starts and ends
Inside an ordinary room, while in the interim

Brimming with illusions, filled with commonplace
Delights that make the days go by, with simple
Arguments and fears, and with the nervous
Inkling of some vague, utopian conceit
Transforming both the landscape and our lives,
Until we look around and find ourselves at home,
But in a wholly different world. And even those
Catastrophes that seemed to alter everything
Seem fleeting, grounded in a natural order
All of us are subject to, and ought to celebrate.
—Yet *why*? That things are temporary doesn't
Render them unreal, unworthy of regretting.
It's not as though the past had never happened:
All those years were real, and their loss was real,
And it *is* sad—I don't know what else to call it.
I'm glad that both of us seem happy. Yet what
Troubles me is just the way what used to be a world
Turned out, in retrospect, to be a state of mind,
And no more tangible than that. And now it's gone,
And in its place I find the image of a process
Of inexorable decay, or of some great unraveling
That drags the houses forward into emptiness
And backwards into pictures of the intervening days
Love pieced together out of nothing. And I'm
Certain that this austere vision finally is true,
And yet it strikes me as too meager to believe.
It comes from much too high above the world
And seems to me too hopeless, too extreme—
But then I found myself one winter afternoon
Remembering a quiet morning in a classroom

And inventing everything again, in ordinary
Terms that seemed to comprehend a childish
Dream of love, and then the loss of love,
And all the intricate years between.

North Point North

IN ITALY

FOR HENRI COLE

1. HOTEL SOLFERINO

I was somewhere else, then here.
I have photographs to prove it, and new clothes.
    Somewhere else: call it an idea
Lingering in the air like the faint smell of rose
    Insensibly near;

    Or call it a small hotel
Towards the end of Via Solferino,
    With a window open to the sun
And the sounds of automobiles on the street below
    And a distant bell.

    Call it any time but now,
Only call it unreal. In time's small room
    Whatever lies beyond its borders
Couldn't have been, like an imaginary perfume
    Nobody knows how

    To even dream of again.
I suppose it was an ordinary day
    In the extraordinary world where
Nothing ever happens, when in something like the way
    A poem begins

I entered upon a street
I'd never imagined before, all the while
        Concealed by that close sense of self
I know now is my true home, and by a passive style
        That seemed to repeat

        My name, that tried to consume
My entire world, that brought me to the entry
        Of a small hotel where an image
Of my own face stared at me from another country,
        From another room.

2. EXPULSION FROM THE GARDEN

It's hard to remember one was ever there,
Or what was supposed to be so great about it.
Each morning a newly minted sun rose
In a new sky, and birdsong filled the air.
There were all these things to name, and no sex.
The children took what God had given them—
A world held in common, a form of life
Without sin or moral complexity,
A vernal paradise complete with snakes—
And sold it all for a song, for the glory
Of the knowledge contained in the fatal apple.
At any rate, that's the official story.

In Masaccio's fresco in the Brancacci Chapel
The figures are smaller than you'd expect

And lack context, and seem all the more tragic.
The Garden is implicit in their faces,
Depicted through the evasive magic
Of the unpresented. Eve's arm is slack
And hides her sex. There isn't much to see
Beyond that, for the important questions,
The questions to which one constantly comes back,
Aren't about their lost, undepicted home,
But the ones framed by their distorted mouths:
What are we now? What will we become?

Think of it as whatever state preceded
The present moment, this prison of the self.
The idea of the Garden is the idea
Of something tangible which has receded
Into stories, into poetry.
As one ages, it becomes less a matter
Of great intervals than of minor moments
Much like today's, which time's strange geometry
Has rendered unreal. And yet the question,
Raised anew each day, is the same one,
Though the person raising it isn't the same:
What am I now? What have I become?

3. DUOMO

Something hung in the air, settled in my mind
And stayed there. I sometimes wonder
What I set about to find, and what intention,

However tentative, hid behind the veil
That evening in the dormitory, and is hiding still
Behind each day's interrogation, each successive station
On this road I've followed now for almost forty years.
It isn't poetry, for the poems are just a pretext
For a condition I have no name for, floating beyond language
Like the thought of heaven, but less defined.

I kept it to myself until I thought it spoke to me
In my own voice, in words in which I recognized my name.
I wasn't there. The streets I'd walked through just a week ago
Were empty, there was silence in the square
In front of the cathedral, and the light in the Galleria
Was the clear light of a dream, of a fixed flame.
The places I had seen were places on a page.
The person I had been was sitting in a room,
Dreaming of a distant city and a different room
And a moment when the world seemed old again, and strange.

I find it hard to talk about myself directly.
The things I say are true, and yet they feel like exercises
In evasion, with the ground shifting beneath my feet
As the subject changes with each changing phrase.
The cathedral wasn't tall, but it dominated the square
Like a Gothic wedding cake, its elaborate facade
Masking a plain interior, much simpler than Chartres' or Notre Dame's.
Standing in the vault I had the sense of being somewhere else,
Of being *someone* else, of floating free of the contingencies
Of personality and circumstance that bore my name.

I went outside and climbed the stairs to the roof.
Behind the spires the old stone shapes gave way to office towers and
    factories
And then the suburbs beyond, all melting into air, into mere air,
Leaving just the earth, and the thought of something watching from afar.
I climbed back down and went inside. The sense of dislocation
That I'd felt at first felt fainter now, as things resumed their proper order.
There were vendors selling guidebooks, and people talking.
Somewhere in the gloom a prayer began. I stared up at the dome
One last time, and then walked out into the sunlight
And the anonymity and freedom of the crowded square.

SONGS OF THE VALLEY

There are two choirs, one poised in space,
Compelled by summer and the noise of cars
Obscured behind the green abundance of the leaves.
The other one is abstract, kept alive by words
Deflected from their courses, gathered
And assembled in the anonymity of someone's room.
Their crescendos mount like mountains of desire,
Like bodies floating through a spectral haze
Of unimagined sounds, until the masks drop,
And the face of winter gazes on the August day
That spans the gap between the unseen and the seen.
The academies of delight seem colder now,
The chancellors of a single thought
Distracted by inchoate swarms of feelings
Streaming like collegians through the hollow colonnades.
Fish swim in the rivers. Olives ripen on the trees.
And the wind comes pouring through the valley
Like the flowing monologue of the mirror,
Celebrating the rocks and hills beyond the window.
The clouds are stones set in the inner sky
Where the nights and days distill their contradictions,
The piano is the minor of a dream, and distant
Fires transmit their codes from ridge to ridge.
It is a pageant of the wistful and the real, sound
And sense, archaic figures and the eyes that see them
In absentia. Morning is a different dream,

Waking to the embarrassment of a face,
To a paradox created in the semblance of a person
Who remains a pessimist of the imagination,
Caught up in the coarse mesh of thought
Through which life flows, and is celebrated.

THE OTHER SIDE OF THE CANYON

In the last crazy afternoon light . . .
—Alfred Kazin

One of the scenes I keep returning to
Is of an airplane gradually descending
Through a sky stretched out above a vacant lot
On the other side of the canyon, where a bunch of guys
Keep yelling to each other as the baseball game wears on
Towards six o'clock, and the waning afternoon
Distills the day into a fluid moment
Flowing with the future and the premise of a life to come.
The days were filled with daydreams of another city
And the artifacts of adolescence:
Camping trips and science fairs and track meets,
Baseball after school, the reveries of physics
And a voice that reached me from across the canyon
While the evening was still full of light
To tell me it was time for dinner, and time to come home.
And all the while the airplanes flew in from the east
Above the table talk and homework and piano lessons
And the dog that kept on barking in the yard.
And when the light had finally emptied from the sky
The moon arose, and then I pulled the curtains
And the room became a globe of lamplight
Which I gathered to myself, lost in the encyclopedia
And at peace in the security of evening, with its quiet promises
Of coming in, and then of leaving home.

*

In a sense each life is merely preparation
For another one, the one implicit
In the step-by-step progression towards some dream deferred
In which each year is homework for the next,
And whose logic only settles into place in retrospect
When all the years have narrowed to a point
From which the rest spread outwards in concentric waves.
They gave me everything I might have wanted,
Everything I'd imagined, from the lights that came alive at evening
To the walk to the hotel at dawn through empty streets.
And when I think of how the future seemed to me at seventeen
There's nothing missing—people recognize my name,
The nights bring music and a kind of peace,
And on these summer mornings sunlight celebrates the rooms.
The window at my desk gives on the tops of trees
Through which the street below is visible,
And in the background I can feel the presence of the lake.
Yet sometimes late at night I think about that voice
Still floating like the moon above the rooftops
And calling me home. My life seems drained,
As though it came to nothing but a catalog of incidents
To be contained between the covers of a book
And then abandoned, installed in someone's library
On a shelf behind a pane of glass.

I wonder if I ever really heard that voice.
A thought creates the settings where it feels at home,
And the facts are less important than the feeling of the words
That spell the future, and that wrote the past.
The half-truths make a ladder to the stars

That no one wants to climb anymore,
For everyone has grown up again, and moved away.
The evening is inscrutable: no magic distance looms,
No fragrance lingers on the skin.
The sky is made of cardboard, the cast is restless and bored,
Waiting in the wings for the performance to begin.
Down in the street some kids are playing soccer
While the sky presides indifferently above.
Is this really how it starts? With a memory of lamplight
Set against a dark background of love? But the ending is alone,
Not in an interesting sense, but just alone.
I write these things and wish that they were mine,
But they're really no one's: the stories they disclose
Are pieced together from the possibilities
I harbor at the center of my heart,
Of things I heard or simply might have heard
And saw or wished I'd seen
Before it was time to come home.

THE PROXIMATE SHORE

It starts in sadness and bewilderment,
The self-reflexive iconography
Of late adolescence, and a moment

When the world dissolves into a fable
Of an alternative geography
Beyond the threshold of the visible.

And the heart is a kind of mute witness,
Abandoning everything for the sake
Of an unimaginable goodness

Making its way across the crowded stage
Of what might have been, leaving in its wake
The anxiety of an empty page.

Thought abhors a vacuum. Out of it came
A partially recognizable shape
Stumbling across a wilderness, whose name,

Obscure at first, was sooner or later
Sure to be revealed, and a landscape
Of imaginary rocks and water

And the dull pastels of the dimly lit
Interior of a gymnasium.
Is art the mirror of its opposite,

Or is the world itself a mimesis?
This afternoon at the symposium
Someone tried to resurrect the thesis

That a poem is a deflected sigh.
And I remembered a day on a beach
Thirty-five years ago, in mid-July,

The summer before I left for college,
With the future hanging just out of reach
And constantly receding, like the edge

Of the water floating across the sand.
Poems are the fruit of the evasions
Of a life spent trying to understand

The vacuum at the center of the heart,
And for all the intricate persuasions
They enlist in the service of their art,

Are finally small, disappointing things.
Yet from them there materializes
A way of life, a way of life that brings

The fleeting pleasures of a vocation
Made up of these constant exercises
In what still passes for celebration,

That began in a mood of hopelessness
On an evening in a dormitory
Years and years ago, and seemed to promise

A respite from disquietude and care,
But that left only the lovely story
Of a bright presence hanging in the air.

DELLIUS' BOAT

In that dark boat, that bears us all away
From here to where no one comes back from ever.
—Horace

So the journey resumes as it began,
With the raw materials of a whole life
Somehow compressed into a brief span
Of years when everything seems obvious,

An indelible period that begins
On a certain day in September,
And that ends on a morning a few years later.
Mostly I seem to remember

Books that felt almost like hymns, for better
Or worse, of passing and regret: Proust,
And *Tender Is the Night*, and "Exile's Letter,"
Which I think I read my freshman year.

The tenses get confused, like those arguments
About life and the imagination
One eventually abandons,
As with each succeeding generation

Adolescence once more finally ends,
This time in a house on a corner
Filled with roommates and girlfriends and ex-girlfriends
And parents and stepparents and ex-wives.

At dusk we strolled through the Illumination,
Through a daze of colored paper lanterns,
And a bandstand on the village green.
The lamps in the leaves threw intricate patterns

Where the next day the families sat about
On folding chairs, while the graduates,
Some of them wearing gowns, and some without,
Wrestled with the dilemma of the Arch.

A commencement speaker from central casting
Told them how to reach the mountaintop,
And then it was all over. We dispersed,
Spurred on by an occasional raindrop,

And though time is ample, with nothing to fear,
The last thought is still one of regret,
Of people borne in a boat, from here
To a place from which no one ever returns.

ILLIERS

FOR SUSAN STEWART

They lie together in the hidden place
Between the bookends, hidden in the heart,
Where time makes of its subjects terms of art:
The hazy children wandering through the forest;
Or the "little phrase," wrung from the purest
Music indistinguishable from space.
The bird that perched and sat above the door.
The cool sunlight on the granary floor.

These things and their negations are all true.
All these are things I know. And what I knew
Is sand, and the hours answer with a chime.
The sin is will: the madness to restore,
The will to what was so indefinite before
It seems a story, painful as a knife
Twisted in the wound, that returned to life
Just once, the once of once upon a time.

CONTEMPORARIES AND ANCESTORS

Sure, some words were spelled differently,
And the clothes and customs weren't the same.
Maybe some of the pets were different too
—The polecat-ferret, the parakeet—
Yet behind the blizzard of appearance
From whence those first impressions came
There was always something constant, and shared.
The stars came out at night, the pale moon rose
To a plaintive melody of care, and what was meant by
Virtue had the virtue of a name
—"Aromatic rose spurred by illusion"—
Like an extended sonnet, whose turn
Seems inexplicable now. I pull them to myself,
That where was once unfurled a glittering display
Of language written like the stars,
A small and truer semblance might unfold.
Let brilliance fall from my consideration,
That the fragrance of some long-forgotten air
Might seize me with a sudden rush, as from a thicket
Birds erupt, and startle through the air,
And vanish in the bright confusion of their cries.
And let the cloak of anonymity descend
Over my heart, upon that bordered, public space
Wherein the figure of the human soul awaits
And in its waiting flourishes and dies, O bear me
From these visions of our common suffering!

*

—But the answer is a pond
In which one's face is barely visible.
The sullen clouds hang low above the trees.
The fields stand as empty as the skies.
Something marvelous is gone—
The intonations of a different form of life
That beckoned from the pages of a prayer book
And the cadences of hymns one heard a century ago.
It was a stronger mode of feeling,
A stranger way of being in the world
That vanished for the sake of an appearance,
A garland of forget-me-nots. Things fall away,
And fall away so quickly. Think of the Ink Spots—
"Whispering Grass" was almost sixty years ago,
But to me it's still a song in high school.
Whitman died how many years before my father's birth?
Eighteen? And Tennyson? There was a common grace,
Sustained by the illusion of a common good,
That shook the souls of fools and geniuses alike.
And though I realize that none of this is true,
The motives seem ingenuous enough:
To place an incoherent dream of aspiration
In the context of an argument I thought I'd understood—
As though the reasoning I'd sought lay dormant
In the dark recesses of some half-forgotten books,
Whose premises were residues of feeling
Tracing out the movements of the intricate
Detritus of a spent imagination, until the clouds lift,
And the sunlight filters through the thin venetian blinds,
And narrows to this small, irreferential space.

Y2K (1933)

The age demanded an image
Of its accelerated grimace . . .
—Ezra Pound

Some of us were tempted to oblige,
Until the aesthetics got so complicated:
Private, yes, but at the same time
Sculpted as from stone and freighted with the
Weight and shape of history, each one
Part of something bigger, something
No one could explain, or even describe.
A change was on the way, eliding outwards
From the chambers of self-doubt into a torchlit Platz
In waves of imagery and rhetoric
That motioned towards some none too distant future
Where a narrow cage awaited, and Cassandra
Practiced the extreme, the fraudulent emotions.

So the image of the age wound down to insects in a jar:
The light flows in, and you can see for miles,
But try to move and something lifeless intervenes.
The truth is on the outside, where the atmosphere is far too
Rarefied to breathe, while here inside the confines
Of our individual lives we reign as kings, as
Kings of the inconsequential. And the soul inscribes its
Shape in the profusion of the sky, yet its reality is
Small, and bounded on all sides

By language writhing with the unrequited
Ache of what was free and fine and
Now surrounds us everywhere, a medium
Too general to inhabit or feel.

"Look," I tell myself, I tell my soul,
"Those sentiments were fine, but they've had their say,
And something stronger is in the air, and you can feel it."
So the fantasy of now sustains an arc of flight
That takes it from a vague, malignant vacuum
To this calm suburban street where on a winter morning
Snow falls as the postman makes his rounds
And something gathers in the corners, something innocent
And evil as a sighing in the sky, insistent
And inert, dragged backwards by a constant
Nagging at the base of the brain, an ill-defined
Unease that hides the horror in the heart, but always working
Towards the future, towards the Führer.

MOORE'S PARADOX

I don't like poems about philosophy,
But then, what is it? Someone
Sees the world dissolving in a well,
Another sees the moving image of eternity
In a shard of time, in what we call a moment.
Are they philosophers? I guess so,
But does it matter? G. E. Moore
Maintained we dream up theories
Incompatible with things we really know, a
Paradox which hardly seems peculiar to our breed.
Poets are worse, or alternately, better
At inhabiting the obviously untrue and
Hoisting flags of speculation in defiance of the real—
In a way that's the point, isn't it?
Whatever holds, whatever occupies the mind
And lingers, and takes flight?

Then from deep within the house
I heard the sound of something I'd forgotten:
Raindrops on the window and the thrashing
Noise the wind makes as it pulses through the trees.
It brought me back to what I meant to say
As time ran out, a mind inside an eggshell boat,
The elements arrayed against it:
Reason as a song, a specious
Music played between the movements of two dreams,
Both dark. I hear the rain.

The silence in the study is complete.
The sentence holds me in its song
Each time I utter it or mentally conceive it,
Calling from a primitive domain
Where time is like a moment
And the clocks stand silent in the chambers,
And it's raining, and I don't believe it.

THEORIES OF PRAYER

The stance is one of supplication, but to whom?
Time pours into the present, while a greater,
Vaguer presence menaces the borders of that country
Whose geography lies entirely within.
Half-hidden trees, half-articulated sounds
And the sympathetic murmur of the heightened mind—
These are the symptoms of an inwardness made visible
In deferential gestures and repeated words.
Come seek me, let the expiation start
The genie said, and for a while the air was
Sweeter with the promise of another life,
An afterlife, all eager to begin.
Yet things are temporary, and the beautiful design
That seemed to lurk behind a fragrant veil
Dissolved, leaving the houses, streets,
The trees, the canyons, even the distant hills,
As they were before.

                  What wilderness resumes,
What world is offered to the milky light
As the air turns vagrant with the scent of spring?
The prayers are possibilities renewed,
Uncertainties restored, which as they cast their shadows
Bring the magic vagueness back to life.
The days were studies in belief,
The evenings like a chamber filled with grace
And buffeted by doubts and dreams

That vanished in the morning, whose uneasy
Presence lingered all the way to school.
It was an incoherent way of living in the world—
Living in the bubble of an adolescent poem
Composed in equal parts of hope and fear
And of a cruelty that conjured up a vision of a
Hell so vivid that the room dissolved. The church retreat
Seems yesterday, but it was forty years ago.
Between, the soul and its surroundings
Came to terms: a few hymns kept their grandeur,
But the rest retreated to the smaller forms
Of happiness and disappointment, to the minor keys
Of a life turned literal.

                    Come walk with me
Along this path that leads us to the lake.
See how the buds look firm, and how these mansions
Filled with furniture and ghosts are tottering past repair.
Look at the golf course, at this lighthouse
Towering above a park where people stroll, and play croquet.
Observe the dogs, the statues by the bridge,
The couples hidden in their thoughts
Yet plain to see, the peaceful absence of complexity
That brings the afternoon to life,
As though mere seeing were a way to pray.
Continue downwards, past the hospital
I visited so many years ago, before things changed
And my life became the one I have today—
Neither good, nor bad, nor something in between,
A fact among facts. See how the lake

At last floats into view, some days a troubled brown
As currents roil the sand, but on this afternoon
A soft, translucent emerald near the shore, and farther out
A darker blue, but still serene.
Unfathomed as an ocean, deep as any dream,
Its shape is that of the horizon, circumscribing nothing
But a vast expanse of water, which extends
As far as I can see, and makes me glad.

STRANGENESS

FOR MARK STRAND

Ariel had mixed thoughts:
The broken century
And the erotics of the paradoxical;
The intimate delusions

And a light, innocuous pretense
Set against the still more fabulous impostors;
The smallest will, beating its wings
Against the cage of space—

These had all become familiar
And unexceptional. We live them,
Live in and through them.
Strangeness lay in ordinary moments

Placed against a background
—Is there another word for "eternity"?—
Of the impersonal: curved space
Foaming with brief particles

As you leave the room.

NORTH POINT NORTH

I

In these I find my calling:
In the shower, in the mirror, in unconscious
Hours spent staring at a screen
At artifacts complete unto themselves.
I think of them as self-sufficient worlds
Where I can sojourn for a while,
Then wake to find the clouds dispersing
And the sidewalks steaming with the
Rain that must have fallen while I stayed inside.
The sun is shining, and the quiet
Doubts are answered with more doubts,
For as the years begin to mirror one another
And the diary in the brain implodes,
What filters through the theories on the page
Is a kind of settledness, an equilibrium
Between the life I have and what time seemed to hold—
These rooms, these poems, these ordinary streets
That spring to life each summer in an intricate construction
Blending failed hopes and present happiness—
Which from the outside seems like self-deception.

There is no end to these reflections,
To their measured music with its dying fall
Wherein the heart and what it seeks are reconciled.
I live them, and as though in gratitude

They shape my days, from morning with its sweetest smile
—Until the hour when sleep blows out the candle.
Between, the present falls away,
And for a while the old romance resumes,
Familiar but unrecognized, an undiscovered place
Concealed within the confines of this room,
That seems at once a form of feeling and a state of grace
Prepared for me, written in my name
Against the time when time has finally merged
These commonplace surroundings with what lies behind the veil.
Leaving behind at least a version of the truth
Composed of what I felt and what I saw outside my window
On a summer morning; melding sound and sense,
A music and a mood, together in a hesitant embrace
That makes them equal at the end.

II

There may be nothing for a poem to change
But an atmosphere: conventional or strange,
Its meaning is enclosed by the perception
—Better, by the misperception—
Of what time held and what the future knew;
Which is to say this very moment.
And yet the promise of a distant
Purpose is what makes each moment new.

There may be nothing for the soul to say
In its defense, except to describe the way

It came to find itself at the impasse
Morning reveals in the glass—
The road that led away from home to here,
That began in wonderment and hope,
But that ended in the long slope
Down to loneliness and the fear of fear.

The casuistry is all in the event,
Contingent on what someone might have meant
Or might still mean. What feels most frightening
Is the thought that when the lightning
Has subsided, and the clearing sky
Appears at last above the stage
To mark the only end of age,
That God, that distant and unseeing eye,

Would see that none of this had ever been:
That none of it, apparent or unseen,
Was ever real, and all the private words,
Which seemed to fill the air like birds
Exploding from the brush, were merely sounds
Without significance or sense,
Inert and dead beneath the dense
Expanse of the earth in its impassive rounds.

There may be no rejoinder to that thought.
There may be nothing that one could have sought
That might have lent the search significance,
Or even a kind of coherence.
Perhaps. Yet closer to me than the grandeur

Of the vast and the uncreated
Is the calm of this belated
Moment in its transitory splendor.

III

Someone asked about the aura of regret
And disappointment that surrounds these poems,
About the private facts those feelings might conceal,
And what their source was in my life.

I said that none of it was personal,
That as lives go my own life was a settled one,
Comprising both successes and misfortunes, the successes
Not especially striking, the misfortunes small.

And yet the question is a real one,
And not for me alone, though certainly for me.
For even if, as Wittgenstein once claimed,
That while the facts may stay the same

And what is true of one is true of both,
The happy and unhappy man inhabit different worlds,
One still would want to know which world this is,
And how that other one could seem so close.

So much of how life feels lies in the phrasing,
In the way a thought starts, then turns back upon itself
Until its question hangs unanswered in the breeze.
Perhaps the sadness is a way of seeming free,

Of denying what can change or disappear,
Of tearing free from circumstance,
As though the soul could only speak out from the
Safety of some private chamber in the air.

Let me try once more. I think the saddest moments
Are the ones that also seem most beautiful,
For the nature of a moment is to fade,
Leaving everything unaltered, and the landscape

Where the light fell as it was before.
And time makes poetry from what it takes away,
And the measure of experience
Is not that it be real, but that it last,

And what one knows is simply what one knew,
And what I want is simply what I had.
These are the premises that structure what I feel,
The axioms that govern my imagination,

And beneath them lies the fear—
Not the fear of the unknown, but the fear of growing old
Unchanged, of looking in the mirror
At a future that repeats itself ad infinitum.

It could be otherwise so easily.
The transience that lectures so insistently of loss
Could speak as clearly of an openness renewed,
A life made sweeter by its changing;

And the shadows of the past
Could seem a shade where one could linger for a while
Before returning to the world, and moving on.
The way would be the same in either case,

Extending for an unknown span of years
Experienced from two perspectives, a familiar course
Accessible to all, yet narrowing,
As the journey nears its end, to one.

The difference isn't in the details
Or the destination, but in how things feel along the road:
The secret of the quest lies all around me,
While what lurks below the surface is another story,

One of no more consequence or import than the last.
What matters isn't what one chances to believe,
But the force of one's attachments,
And instead of looking for an answer in a dream

Set aside the question, let the songs continue
Going through the motions of the days
And waking every morning to this single world,
Whether in regret, or in celebration.

IV

Each day begins as yesterday began:
A cat in silhouette in the dim light
Of what the morning holds—

Breakfast and *The New York Times*, a man
Taking a shower, a poem taking flight
As a state of mind unfolds
So unpredictably.
Through the hot summer air
I walk to a building where
I give a lecture on philosophy

In the strict sense; then go home to the cat.
A narrow life; or put another way,
A life whose facts can all
Be written on a page, the narrow format
Of this tiny novel of a day,
Ulysses written small,
A diary so deep
Its rhythms seem unreal:
A solitary meal.
Some records or a movie. And then sleep.

V

At the ending of the remake of *The Thing*
Kurt Russell and one other guy
Are all that's left of what had been the crew
Of an Antarctic outpost. Some horrifying presence
—Some protean *thing*—establishes itself
Inside the person of an ordinary man
And then, without a warning, erupts in devastation.
The two survivors eye each other slowly,

Neither knowing whether one of them
Still holds the horror. "What do we do now?"
The second asks, and Russell says,
"Let's see what happens," and the movie ends.

"Horror" is too strong, but substitute the fear
I spoke about before, and the scene is apt.
I don't know, as no one really knows,
What might lie waiting in the years to come,
But sometimes when the question touches me I feel afraid—
Not of age, but an age that seems a prolongation of this afternoon,
That looks ahead, and looks instead into itself.
This is the fear that draws me back inside:
That this is all there is, that what I hold so easily
Will vanish soon, and nothing like it will be given me again.
The days will linger and the nights rehearse themselves
Until the secret of my life has finally emerged—
Not in devastation, but in a long decline
That leads at least as surely to a single end.

And then I turn away and see the sky
That soars above the streets of North Point North,
Reducing everyone to anonymity, an anonymity
In which I find a kind of possibility, a kind of freedom
As the world—the only world—rolls on its way,
Oblivious to anything I might say, or that might happen in a poem.
A poem can seize and hold a moment fast, yet it can
Limit what there is to feel, and stake a distance from the world.
The neighborhood around me wakes each day to lives
No different than my own, lives harboring the same ambitions

And regrets, but living on the humbler stuff of happiness.
The disappointments come and go; what stays
Is part of an abiding presence, human and serene.
The houses wait unquestioning in the light
Of an approaching summer evening, while a vast
Contentment answers from the air.
I think I know where this is going to end,
But still my pleasure is to wait—
Not wait, perhaps, for anything within,
But for what lies outside. Let's see what happens.

GIL'S CAFE

For now the kingdom feels sufficient and complete,
And summer seems to flow through everything:
A girl slides by on roller blades,
The flags flap on the flagpoles, and across the street
The afternoon holds court at Gil's Cafe.
There is this sense of plenitude and peace
And of the presence of the world—
Wasps on the driveway, and purple flowers on the trees,
And a bicycle goes rolling down the hill;
And at length it starts to deepen and increase.

And even as it deepens something turns away,
As though the day were the reflection of a purer day
In which the summer's measures never ended.
The eye that seeks it fills the universe with shapes,
A fabulist, an inquisitor of space
Removed from life by dreams of something other than this life,
Distracted by the bare idea of heaven,
Suspended in the earthly heaven of this afternoon
As off the lake a light breeze blows
And all there is to see lies dormant in the sun.

The sun shines on the houses and the churches and the schools,
On restaurants and parks, on marriages and love affairs,
The playground with its monkey bars and slides,
The bench where someone sits and thinks about the future,
The accident in which a person's life abruptly ends.

The world is like the fiction of a face,
Which tries to hide the emptiness behind a smile
Yet seems so beautiful—insignificant,
And like everything on which the sunlight falls
Impermanent, but enough for a while.

Sally's Hair

(2006)

THE PERFECT LIFE

I have a perfect life. It isn't much,
But it's enough for me. It keeps me alive
And happy in a vague way: no disappointments
On the near horizon, no pangs of doubt;
Looking forward in anticipation, looking back
In satisfaction at the conclusion of each day.
I heed the promptings of my inner voice,
And what I hear is comforting, full of reassurance
For my own powers and innate superiority—the fake
Security of someone in the grip of a delusion,
In denial, climbing ever taller towers
Like a tiny tyrant looking on his little kingdom
With a secret smile, while all the while

Time lies in wait. And what feels ample now
Turns colorless and cold, and what seems beautiful
And strong becomes an object of indifference
Reaching out to no one, as later middle age
Turns old, and the strength is gone.
Right now the moments yield to me sweet
Feelings of contentment, but the human
Dies, and what I take for granted bears a name
To be forgotten soon, as the things I know
Turn into unfamiliar faces
In a strange room, leaving merely
A blank space, like a hole left in the wake
Of a perfect life, which closes over.

PIRANESI'S KEYHOLE

Here it is then: no constraints,
A future that extends as far as I can see,
As far as I can stand it. Follow me
Along the path of my ambition, through a maze of days
That make up what I want to call my life. Come with me
Of an evening, when the day is at its clearest,
Or a morning when its promise still feels immanent and new.
Be patient. Sit motionless before a page
That holds the image of a face, its questions
Answered by the May sky's deepest blue;
Or put it down to age, or to the way time feels as it passes.
I kept these thoughts contained for over fifty years,
Concealed in what I thought of as a home,
One thousands of miles away, which as its spell broke
Pressed into my consciousness a sense of being
Utterly alone, and in that loneliness completely free,
Untamed by time's constraints or by a world
Of mere seeming, a place of pseudomemories
In which the past is ashes and tomorrow is a wilderness
Of drugs and dreams and trees like clouds and clouds like trees—
A place of air, where everything occurs by choice
In the space of a few minutes; where songs go on forever
And transport me to the threshold of an antiworld
Of no more substance than the words that give it voice, unfolding
At the stately pace of a recitative. Bear with me now,

*

For if you ask how much of this I literally believe,
I don't know what to say—not much, I guess.
I know though that I love the way it passes, as it changes
Boredom to a smile and makes the air seem sweeter while it lasts.
Is it so terrible to try to keep the world at bay,
To treat it as an exercise in make-believe? Some say so,
But to me what matters is the going back and forth
Between two different minds, both incomplete, the liberty to disappear
Into the freedom of a daydream or the freedom of the street.
And when I question what that anonymity might mean
I see a nothingness of sky above the dome of a cathedral,
Or the ruins of some villa overrun with weeds;
I see through Piranesi's Keyhole the hallucination of St. Peter's
Floating in a space and time beyond a corridor of trees,
Or hear the sound of voices I can't recognize in what used to be my home.
There is a place existing only in the mind, or minds,
Approachable through memory or art, an aesthetic counterpart
Of that imaginary world Kant called the Realm of Ends,
That answers only to the laws of its creation. It begins,
If it begins anywhere, in childhood—in a story out of Poe,
Or in a church, or in a private moment glowing with the sense,
Not so much of another life, as that this one is wanting—
Which is also where it ends. We're grown-ups now,
Long past the need for what the stories told us, for a *somewhere else*
Beyond the tangible realities of daily life, beyond the veil.
I know. Yet it isn't in the end a matter of belief, but of an impulse
Rooted in experience, too indeterminate to be a thought,
That says you have to go there though you know it isn't true.

*

—Which is where I started: with a future at my fingertips,
Permissions granted, free to chart the terms of an existence
"Loos'd of limits and imaginary lines." And for a time
I went along with it, enchanted by its promises of a liberty
Of thought and purpose, purpose flowing into action
In a synthesis of feeling and idea, mind and heart. And in a way
Its promises came true, though not the way I'd wanted:
No imaginary lines impede me, nothing intervenes
Between my life as I conceive it and its presence on the page,
Unburdened by the facts of getting older. You see,
I knew the place beyond the keyhole was a figment of my mind,
Albeit one whose fiction was created in my heart;
But what I didn't realize was that the mind containing it
Was unreal too, the specter of a speech delivered from a stage.
And just as one is a creation not to be believed,
So too the soul, for what it glimpses through the aperture of art
Is Berkeley's world, existing simply as perceived,
A haven for the eye that seeks it or the vagrant self
That looks around and tries to call it home,
That celebrates the freedom of its Realm of One,
A freedom purchased at the price of unreality. Who cares
What I believe or don't believe? This voice that speaks to you
Isn't the voice of a person, but the subject of a reverie.
I wish—it started with a wish—at this late hour
I could find a different way of talking, one embodying the life
Of something like a person in an ordinary world;
That I could find a way to place that life in context,
Showing it both as it is and as it wants to be—
But that will have to wait, for having come full circle
And remaining of two minds, I take my leave.

AUBADE

It's early, but I recognize this place.
I recognize the feeling, after an endless
Week of mornings in America, of returning
To the home one never really leaves,
Mired in its routines. I walk to what I try to
Tell myself is work, entering at the end of the day
The same room, like the man in *Dead of Night*—
The dinner, the DVD from Netflix,
The drink before I go to sleep and wake alone
In the dead of night like Philip Larkin
Groping through the dark at 4 a.m. to piss,
At home in the reality of growing old
Without ever growing up. I finally get up
An hour later, run, eat breakfast, read and write—
A man whose country is a state of mind,
A community of one preoccupied with time,
Leaving me with nothing much to do
But to write it off to experience—the experience
Of a rudimentary consciousness at 5 a.m.,
Aware of nothing but the drone
Of its own voice and a visual field
Composed of dogs and joggers in a park.

WHEN THERE WAS TIME

Physics and—what?—existentialism?
Guitar heroes and singer-songwriters
And death? You were supposed to write poems
Breath by breath, movies were as serious

As novels, and tomorrow was the name
Of a different kind of life, a life
Beyond imagining, hiding in the
Darkness behind the adolescent sun.

The same sun rolled like clockwork through the sky,
Monitoring the road to who knew where,
That trailed off into the shrubbery.
And there was time to find that road again,

To follow its invisible design
And argument, preparing for a place
Of nuance, shadow, and complexity,
Where adolescence was supposed to end.

Who'd want to go there now? There's *always* time,
But when I think about the future now,
It's of a world already done, without
The promise or the threat of difference.

Coming out of a movie (*Best in Show*)
This afternoon, near the corner where the
Oriental Pharmacy used to be,
It seemed to me I'd lived there all my life:

That the theories were all formulated,
The songs all written and sung, and that time—
Not the time of the nostalgias but the
Time of history—had come to an end.

I know that this is age, and only age.
Why should the way time felt when one was young
Change how it feels today, with everything
So static, with the afternoon so still?

I want the darkness back, both in the sky
And here in my heart, that it might remain
Uncharted, still a stranger to itself,
Oblivious of what it was, and change.

THE MIDDLE OF EXPERIENCE

My fear and my ambition: that my life
Remain the same, unchanging in its versions,
Constant as the street I lived on where the
Houses bode their dreams beneath a California sky.
That place is at the heart of what I mean,
Yet when I ask myself when I'll return to it again
The question seems more urgent than the answer,
Coming, as it does, at the end of something—poetry?—
Composed of endless summer afternoons
I can't imagine anymore, and fictions that created
Fictions of their own, yet somehow told
A story of a life indefinite as life,
Happening as it passes, leaving in its wake
An ease of mind and clarity of heart
Like a beautiful day. You want to bask in it,
Which is where you start: the middle of experience,
In a particular place, at a certain age—
In my case in Milwaukee, fifty-six,
My father dead just short of ninety-two,
The house in San Diego sold.

That house was *unbelievable*:
The flyers, when the stuff inside was sold,
Described it as a "decorator's house"—
The rooms like jewel boxes or the interior
Of a Fabergé egg, designed to conceal the facts
Of being old, the boredom and the pain,

The minor pleasures of anticipation or a lovely day,
The chair in which he sat for hours following the light,
Kept company by his catalogs and cat.
After my mother died I wrote a poem
About the presence of a vast, inhuman world
Hidden behind our lives, as if a thing too close to see
Might finally be made visible in death.
Yet this time nothing seemed revealed: the
Neighbors kept their counsel while the realtors came and went
Beneath the flat blue sky I'd known since childhood;
The hospice overlooking Mission Valley
Kept its secret from the warm December day;
The new year promised a "renewal of experience,"
An idea I've never understood.

I wonder if that thought has less to do
With feeling than a sense of place, a sense that
Comes to you the way ideas usually do—
Between breaths, or in the shower,
Or on a walk around the neighborhoods
On a cool day in early spring. That can't be right;
The sense is of an *absence* of a place, a freedom
From constraint, the freedom of a part of me
Inhabiting this poem, and a part I left at home.
I like the image of a lime-green sky
Above a house two thousand miles away,
But distance doesn't matter, and the color—well,
It pleases me, that's all. The lights were on,
The keys were in the kitchen as I closed the door
On what once had been my life, that it might start again—

As though each day were a departure
And forgetting were the real renewal of experience,
Making the commonplace seem strange
And taking me to a place I'd been
So many times before, for the first time.

COLLECTED POEMS

small war on the heels of small / war
—Robert Lowell

I think they may be adequate for now,
With summer finally in full swing
As imperceptibly the days begin to shrink.
Each spring I wonder what I'll find
When I return to them again—this year it was a war
That wasn't actually a war, a lie made visible—
And how blind intuitions might be built up into facts
That someone else might think to feel and read.
The signs are everywhere, implicit in the sky,
The trees, the houses on the street I walk along to work
(The walking *is* the work), when something that I see
Or half-remember gets repeated from inside,
Finds its measure, and in settling inward settles into place.
They're how I wander through a day, wondering at its
Spaciousness, finding in its anonymity
These traces of my name, in its impersonality
These ways to see myself—hearing in the syllables of the
Leaves the lyrics of a song; seeing in the clouds
A human face, another lie made visible.

Word by word and war by war—
What makes one possible sustains the other too:
The urge to change, the power to deceive,
To fabricate a version of the world
Not as it is, but as someone imagines it to be.
The aim is not to say what happened

But to forge a monument by force, deploying
All the subtlety and weapons of the will
And leaving something broken in its wake: the simple truth
As it appeared in school each day; the simple self
That wrote it down, before it all became a wilderness
Where what's still left of them still wander,
Looking for each other, through a mutual memory
Of something irrecoverable beneath these
Shifting sands of spoken and unspoken words.

I used to think there was a different way,
A less insistent one, accepting what it finds
Without revising it, without the specious clarity
And authority of art, and its pervasive
Atmosphere of will. But that turned out to be a style too,
A sweeter one perhaps, yet just as artificial in the end.
The point is general, not confined to art: to make
Is to destroy; to act is to replace what would have been
With something signed, that bears a name. When I was a boy
I thought a life just happened, or was there to find.
Wars were aberrations. Poems were another generation's.
I didn't realize you made it up, you made *them* up,
And that the self was not an object but an act,
A sequence of decisions bound together by a noun
But with the feel of a fact. I wonder where that leaves me—
Hanging on a whim, on what I write? I hope not.
What the urge to dominate the world, the place, the page
Eventually becomes is just a human figure
On a summer afternoon, smiling at what happens,
Anxious for the future and the slope of age.
I think I'm done for now. It remains to save the file,
Close the notebook, and let evening come.

21.1

What I remember are the cinders and the starter's gun,
The lunging forward from a crouch, the power of acceleration
And the lengthening strides, the sense of isolation
And exhilaration as you pulled away, the glory at the tape.

I never really got it back after I pulled my thigh my sophomore year.
I still won races, lettered and was captain of the team,
But instead of breaking free there was a feeling of constraint,
Of being pretty good, but basically second-rate—

Which Vernus Ragsdale definitely was not. When he was eligible
(He was ineligible a lot) no one in the city could come close—
No one in the country pretty much, for this was California. We had our
Meet with Lincoln early in the spring, and he was cleared to run.

I was running the 220 (which I seldom ran) and in the outside lane,
With Ragsdale in lane one. *The stretch, the set, the gun—*
And suddenly the speed came flowing back as I was flying through the turn
And all alone before I hit the tape with no one else in sight.

Friends said he looked as though he'd seen a ghost (a fleet white one).
The atmosphere of puzzlement and disbelief gave way to
Chaos and delirium when they announced the national record time
Of 21.1 and I stood stunned and silent in a short-lived daze—

Short-lived because the explanation rapidly emerged:
They'd put us in the quarter-mile staggers by mistake, to be made up
Around two turns, not one. I'd had a huge head start on
Everyone, on Ragsdale on the inside most of all. By the meet's end

Lincoln was so far ahead they didn't even bother to rerun the race,
And so we ran the relay, lost, and everyone went home—
Leaving me wistful and amused and brooding on the memory
Of my moment in what was now a slowly setting sun.

There's a story that I read my freshman year in college
Called "The Eighty-Yard Run," by Irwin Shaw. It's about a football player
Who makes a perfect run one afternoon and feels a heightened sense of
Possibility and life: the warmth of flannel on his skin, the three cold
    drinks of water,

The first kiss of the woman who is going to be his wife. All lies before him,
Only he never measures up: gradually at first, and then more steeply,
It's a long decline from there, until he finds himself years later on that
Football field again, a traveling salesman selling cut-rate suits.

I'm not immune to sentimental cautionary tales: the opening door
That turns out to have long been shut; the promissory moment,
Savored at the time, with which the present only pales by comparison,
That tinctures what comes later with regret. I'm safe from that—

Track wasn't everything, but even minor triumphs
Take on mythical proportions in our lives. Yet since *my* heightened
    moment
Was a bogus one, I can't look back on it with disappointment
At the way my life has gone since then. Perhaps all public victories

Are in some sense undeserved, constructed out of luck
Or friends or how you happened to feel that day. But mine took off
    its mask
Almost as soon as it was over, long before it had the chance
To seem to settle into fact. I'm human though: sometimes I like to

Fantasize that it had all been true, or had been *taken* to be true—
The first of an unbroken string of triumphs stretching through to college
Real life, and right down to today. I ran that race in 1962,
The year *The Man Who Shot Liberty Valance* was released,

A film about a man whose whole career was built upon a lie.
James Stewart thinks he killed—and everyone *believes* he killed—
Lee Marvin, the eponymous bad guy, although he never actually killed
    anyone at all:
John Wayne had shadowed him and fired the fatal shot,

Yet governor, senator, ambassador, and senator again
All followed on his reputation. He tries at last to set the record straight
—The movie's mostly one long flashback of what happened—
But the editor to whom he tells the real story throws away his notes:

"When the legend becomes fact," he orders, "print the legend,"
As the music soars and draws the veil upon the myth of the Old West.
Print the legend: I'd like to think that's what my story was,
Since for a moment everyone believed that it was true—

But then it wasn't anymore. Yet it's my pleasure to pretend
It could have been: when Willis Bouchey at the end affirms the fairy tale
With "Nothing's too good for the man who shot Liberty Valance,"
I hear in my imagination "who beat Vernus Ragsdale."

SALLY'S HAIR

It's like living in a light bulb, with the leaves
Like filaments and the sky a shell of thin, transparent glass
Enclosing the late heaven of a summer day, a canopy
Of incandescent blue above the dappled sunlight golden on the grass.

I took the train back from Poughkeepsie to New York
And in the Port Authority, there at the Suburban Transit window,
She asked, "Is this the bus to Princeton?"—which it was.
"Do you know Geoffrey Love?" I said I did. She had the blondest hair

Which fell across her shoulders, and a dress of almost phosphorescent
    blue.
She liked Ayn Rand. We went down to the Village for a drink,
Where I contrived to miss the last bus to New Jersey, and at 3 a.m. we
Walked around and found a cheap hotel I hadn't enough money for

And fooled around on its dilapidated couch. An early morning bus
(She'd come to see her brother), dinner plans and missed connections
And a message on his door about the Jersey shore. Next day
A summer dormitory room, my roommates gone: "Are you," she asked,

"A hedonist?" I guessed so. Then she had to catch her plane.
Sally—Sally Roche. She called that night from Florida,
And then I never heard from her again. I wonder where she is now,
Who she is now. That was thirty-seven years ago

And I'm too old to be surprised again. The days are open,
Life conceals no depths, no mysteries, the sky is everywhere,
The leaves are all ablaze with light, the blond light
Of a summer afternoon that made me think again of Sally's hair.

PROUST

I don't remember how it started. In high school
I'd devoured "modern fiction"—Dostoevsky,
Joyce and Woolf, Fitzgerald, Faulkner, Hemingway
And Lewis (oops!)—but still no poetry. Why don't you
Read some Thomas Hardy? asked my English teacher.
Yet I persevered, and by the end of my third year in college
Reached the mountain waiting at the end. And thus
Began the summer of *Swann's Way, Within a Budding Grove,*
The Guermantes Way and half of *Cities of the Plain.*
I'd read them in my bedroom, on our patio in San Diego
Where my progress was the progress of a cloud
Across the endlessly receding skies above Combray.
The sentences, as you can see, proceeded at their pace,
The pace of life: I broke up with my girlfriend;
Poetry took some poems of mine; my summer job
Was cleaning floors in local schools; a letter from New York
Arrived to tell me Frank O'Hara (whom I'd met at
Dinner just three months before) was dead.
The pages turned: Odette, Gilberte, the Jockey Club
Assumed their places like the place-names on the rail line.
I was young. I tried to find my story written in the years
To come, but everything I found was something that I'd read,
Whose *raison d'être* was the imperative of reading on—
And so I left it all to chance, as summer ended
With the pollination dance of Charlus and Jupien.

*

Fall came, my final college year. I set his books aside
But found a surrogate, George Painter's marvelous biography
That focused on the same world through a different lens.
One night I let a Vox Box of French chamber music—Debussy,
Ravel, Fauré and Frank—play on and on throughout the night
As in the darkness of my dormitory room I dreamed about
That soundless room at 44 rue Hamelin. Then winter came,
And spring, and then commencement brought an end
To my "bright college years" and I went back to California,
Only to resume his endless monographs on Albertine and jealousy,
The Captive and *The Sweet Cheat Gone*. Life channeled art:
I fell in love and wrote my first long poem. Somehow I'd stumbled
Into graduate school, and soon the time had come for me to leave.
I read *The Past Recaptured* on the plane and on a bench in Harvard Yard
And on a Greyhound to New York to ship my things and visit John.
I told him I was nearly done. "This must be a tender moment,"
He replied. "Do you want to be alone?" I said I didn't,
So we went downstairs where I could meet "Old Stanley" Kunitz
(Old!—he's ninety-nine now; this was almost forty years ago)
At a party at the Cavallons'. The book ends with a party. Russell Baker,
When he'd finished, wrote a column in the *Times* that gave away the
    ending:
"There's this big party and everybody has gotten a lot older,"
Which about sums it up. Upstairs at John's I finally
Gained the final words—"so widely separated from one another
In Time."—reread them once or twice, and closed the book.

It changes you. You're a different person by the end,
If only since it takes so long to read. I used to tell myself
I'd read it one more time before I died, but long ago

I realized I won't. And so the boxed three volume set
I got how many years ago? sits on the shelf, a mute reproach.
Where did I find the energy, the time? A new translation
Of *Swann's Way* came out last year. I think I'll take it to Berlin—
I'm surely up to that, I'd like to think. Sometimes I take the old one down
And read the coda, where the narrator, now writing in the present,
Wakes at dawn and goes out to the park. The gym is closed
For renovations, so I've started getting up at 5 a.m. and running in Lake
     Park,
Milwaukee's own Bois de Boulogne, but on a smaller scale. "Marcel"
Is horrified by what he sees, by how it differs from the world that he
     recalls
—The hats, the clothes, the motorcars, the ripples on the real lake—
And yet what strikes me is how innocent it seems: the mist upon the
     golf course
And the white moon hanging in a pale sky still rosy in the east.
There's no one there. The world is waiting. Time feels like a structure
Waiting to be filled with scenes from the generic lives
We all lead, interchangeable, yet every one a story to itself
Whose truth lies in its style, the passage of that life
From childhood to here, complete with names and places
Fleshing out a novel's worth of days. No matter how detailed,
They disappear, and nothing can convey the simple truth
Of what each one was like, that sense of something now as
Indeterminate and fugitive, alas, as the years.

16A:

The apartment on Francis Avenue
We lived in for three years in graduate school
In the nicest—or maybe second nicest—part of Cambridge,
On the third floor of Joe and Annie's house

Just up the street from the Divinity School.
John Kenneth Galbraith lived next door,
Julia Child's Kitchen was across a backyard fence
I'd hang around trying to look hungry,

And emulating her we rented a meat locker at Savenor's,
Where I'd stop to pick up a pot roast or a steak
Before coming home to Jeepers waiting for me in the window.
Everything happened then, in two or three years

That seemed a lifetime at the time:
The War and SDS and music; the confusion in the streets
And Nixon; poetry and art and science, philosophy and immunology,
The dinners at Bill and Willy's loft in Soho—

Yet what still stays with me is the summer of 1973,
The summer before we moved to Milwaukee, with my dissertation done
And time to kill, suspended on the brink of real life.
I would read the first draft of "Self-Portrait"

John had let me copy, and *Gravity's Rainbow*,
And every afternoon I'd ride my bike to Bob's house
Where I'd watch the hearings on TV. And on a Saturday in June,
With the living room awash in the late yellow light

That filtered through the western dormer window,
We watched, just out of curiosity, this horse I'd read about
—And what I knew about the Sport of Kings was nil—
Turn what till then had been an ordinary day

Into one as permanent as anything in sports or art or life,
As Secretariat came flying through the turn with the announcer crying
"He's all *alone*—he's moving like a *tremendous machine*,"
And Susan shouting "Look at that horse! Look at that horse!"

The summer sort of dribbled away. We took a last trip to New York,
John and Rebecca stopped over on their way to somewhere,
James and Lisa too, whom I hadn't seen in years,
And then we packed our stuff and took the cat and drove away.

Nixon hung on for a while, and then—but that's history,
Real history, not this private kind that monitors the unimportant
For what changes, for what doesn't change. Here I am,
Living in Milwaukee twenty-nine years later.

Susan lives about a mile away, and just last Saturday
The latest wonder horse, War Emblem, stumbled in the Belmont Stakes.
What *makes* a life, if not the places and the things that make it up?
I know that I exist, but what about that place we lived? Is it still real?

—Of course it is. It just gets harder to see
As time goes by, but it's still all there. Last month in Rome
The first thing Lisa said was that I looked just like myself, but with
        white hair.
And there it is: look at the tiny strawberries and the

Flowers blooming in the garden of the house next door.
Look at John Dean, still testifying on that little screen, and Rogers,
Who died in May, still talking in our small blue dining room.
Look at Savenor's, the unkempt lawn, the mailbox by the back porch,

Jeepers waiting for me in the window. Look at that horse!

HAMLET

... a divinity that shapes our ends.

It was math and physics all the way,
The subjects of the life that I'd designed
In high school, that carried me away,
A callow California youth with Eastern dreams,
From home. The thought of something abstract
And aloof, penetrating to the heart of the unknown
And consigning everything else to the realm of unreality—
I didn't believe it then and don't believe it now,
Yet something in the fantasy felt so complete,
So like the lyrics of a song that spoke to me alone,
I bought it. How quaint that vision seems now
And mundane the truth: instead of paradox and mystery
And heroic flights of speculation that came true,
You had to start with classical mechanics and a lab;
Instead of number theory and the satisfactions
Of the private proof, a class of prodigies manqué
Made jokes in mathematics that I didn't get.
And there were problems with the style,
The attitudes, the clothes, for this was 1963,
The future waiting in the wings and practically on stage—
The Beatles and Bob Dylan and Ali, né Cassius Clay,
Who from the distance of today look like clichés of history,
But at the time seemed more like strangers in the
Opening pages of a story I was learning how to write.
The new year brought Ed Sullivan and track,

But what with winter and the little indoor track
My times were never close to what I'd run in high school.
I started hanging out across the hall—they seemed, I guess,
More "Eastern" than my roommates, closer to the picture of myself
That called me in the first place: Norwich, Vermont,
The Main Line and St. George's, and (I guess it figured)
A prospective civil engineer. And then there was New York:
I'd been in once or twice, though not for dinner,
So when James suggested Richard Burton's *Hamlet*
At the Lunt-Fontanne I fell right in. We went to dinner
At a place on Forty-sixth Street called Del Pezzo,
Up some steps and with bay windows and a chandelier.
We ordered saltimbocca and drank Soave Bolla
As I listened, Ripley-like, to recollections of three-hour
Lunches at a restaurant on a beach somewhere near Rome.
And then the lights went down, and when at last
The ghost had vanished, Burton strode upon the stage.
It was, I think, the first "bare" *Hamlet*—Hamlet
In a turtleneck, the rest in street clothes, virtually no scenery—
Leaving nothing but the structure of the play, and voices,
Burton's resonant and strong yet trembling on the brink of
Breaking, as for hours, from the first *I know not seems* until
The rest is silence, he compelled the stage. And then,
The bodies everywhere, the theater went black and we went
Somewhere for a drink and took the last bus home—

For by then I'd come to think of it as home.
By next fall everything had changed. My roommates
Were the former guys across the hall, sans engineer.
In San Diego Mr. Weisbrod from the science fair

Was appalled, as math and physics disappeared,
Supplanted by philosophy. A letter from the track coach
Lay unanswered by an ashtray, and I took a course
From Carlos Baker, Hemingway's biographer, in which I
First read modern poetry—*The Waste Land*, Moore, *The Cantos*,
Frost and Yeats—and dreamed that I might do that too.
I wish I knew what happened. Was the change
The outward resolution of some inner struggle
Going on since childhood, or just a symptom of the times?
So much of what we're pleased to call our lives
Is random, yet we take them at face value,
Linking up the dots. Feeling out of it one evening,
Staring at our Trenton junk store chandelier,
I started a pastiche of Frost ("In the mists of the fall . . .")
And even tried to write a play about a deadly clock
Styled on Edward Albee's now (alas) forgotten *Tiny Alice*,
The object of another Broadway interlude, this time a matinee.
Hamlet was forgotten. Pound and Eliot gave way
To Charles Olson and the dogmas of projective verse,
To Robert Duncan and the egotistical sublime,
And finally to "the Poets of the New York School,"
Whose easy freedom and deflationary seriousness combined
To generate what seemed to me a tangible and abstract beauty
As meanwhile, in parallel, my picture of myself evolved
From California science whiz into the impeccable habitué
Of a Fitzgerald fantasy. It became a kind of hobby:
Self-invention, the attempt to realize some juvenile ideal
I cringe to think of now, playing back and forth
Between the guise of the artiste and of the silly little snob,
A pose I like to think of as redeemed (just barely) by a

Certain underlying earnestness. Perhaps I'm being too harsh—
I was serious about the path I'd chosen, one I've
Followed now for forty years. What life worth living
Isn't shaky at the outset, given to exaggerations and false starts
Before it finds its way? Those ludicrous personae were
A passing phase, and by my senior year whatever they'd concealed
Had finally settled into second nature. I'd go on,
But let me leave it there for now. My life after college
(Cf. "16A:" and "Falling Water") more or less continued on the
Course I'd set there, mixing poetry and philosophy
In roughly equal parts, vocation and career. My days
Are all about the same: some language, thought and feeling
And the boredom of the nearly empty day, calling on my
Memory and imagination to compel the hours, from morning
Through the doldrums of the afternoon and into early
Evening, sitting here alone and staring at a page.

You're probably wondering what provoked all this.
For years I'd heard they'd filmed a performance of the play,
To be shown just once and then (supposedly) destroyed.
Browsing on the Web about a month ago I entered,
Out of curiosity, "Richard Burton's Hamlet" into Google.
Up it came, available from Amazon on DVD (apparently
Two copies had survived). I ordered it immediately,
Went out and bought a player (plus a new TV) and watched it
Friday evening, calling up the ghosts of forty years ago.
I'd misremembered one or two details—it was a V-neck,
Not a turtleneck, at least that night—but Burton was
As I'd remembered him, incredible, his powers at their peak,
Just after Antony and Arthur and before the roles

Of Beckett, Reverend Shannon, Alec Leamas, George;
Before the dissolution and decline and early death.
Some nights I feel haunted by the ghost of mathematics,
Wondering what killed it off. I think my life began to change
Just after that performance in New York. Could *that* have been the
Catalyst—a life of words created by a play about a character
Whose whole reality is words? It's nice to speculate,
And yet it's just too facile, for the truth was much more
Gradual and difficult to see, if there to see at all.
We like to think they're up to us, our lives, but by the time we
Glimpse the possibility of changing it's already happened,
Governed by, in Larkin's phrase, what something hidden from us chose
And which, for all we know, might just as well have been the stars.
That adolescent image of myself dissolved, to be replaced by—
By what? I doubt those pictures we create are ever true—
Isn't that the moral to be drawn from this most human of the plays?
It isn't merely the ability to choose, but agency itself—
The thought that we're in charge, and that tomorrow mirrors our
Designs—that lies in ruins on the stage. It isn't just the
Life of a particular young man, but something like the very
Image of the human that dissolves into a mindless anonymity,
Dick Diver disappearing at the end of *Tender Is the Night*
Into the little towns of upper New York State.
I know of course I'm overacting. Burton did it too,
Yet left a residue of truth, and watching him last Friday
I began to realize there'd been no real change,
But just a surface alteration. Sometimes I wonder if this
Isn't just my high-school vision in disguise, a naive
Fantasy of knowledge that survived instead as art—
Aloof, couched in the language of abstraction, flirting

Now and then with the unknown, pushing everything else aside.
This place that I've created has the weight and feel of home,
And yet there's nothing tangible to see. And so I
Bide my time, living in a poem whose backdrop
Is the wilderness of science, an impersonal universe
Where no one's waiting and our aspirations end.
Take up the bodies, for the rest is silence.

Ninety-Fifth Street

(2009)

CHESTER

*Wallace Stevens is beyond fathoming, he is so strange; it is as if
he had a morbid secret he would rather perish than disclose . . .*
   —Marianne Moore to William Carlos Williams

Another day, which is usually how they come:
A cat at the foot of the bed, noncommittal
In its blankness of mind, with the morning light
Slowly filling the room, and fragmentary
Memories of last night's video and phone calls.
It is a feeling of sufficiency, one menaced
By the fear of some vague lack, of a simplicity
Of self, a self without a soul, the nagging fear
Of being someone to whom nothing ever happens.
Thus the fantasy of the narrative behind the story,
Of the half-concealed life that lies beneath
The ordinary one, made up of ordinary mornings
More alike in how they feel than what they say.
They seem like luxuries of consciousness,
Like second thoughts that complicate the time
One simply wastes. And why not? Mere being
Is supposed to be enough, without the intricate
Evasions of a mystery or offstage tragedy.
Evenings follow on the afternoons, lingering in
The living room and listening to the stereo
While Peggy Lee sings "Is That All There Is?"
Amid the morning papers and the usual

Ghosts keeping you company, but just for a while.
The true soul is the one that flickers in the eyes
Of an animal, like a cat that lifts its head and yawns
And looks at you, and then goes back to sleep.

ON HAPPINESS

It's a simple question, and I even know what it is
Until you ask me, as Augustine said of time.
It's either too commonplace or too rare, an esoteric condition
You could spend your life attaining, or a waste of time.

Plato thought of it as a kind of balance in the soul
Between its three parts (though he called it something else),
And Freud thought along the same lines, in his role
As the first happiness therapist, only called it unhappiness

Of the ordinary kind. Wittgenstein said the happy
And unhappy man inhabit two completely different worlds,
While Mill equated it with pleasures of all kinds,
From high to low, from the pleasure mirrored in a young girl's

Smile to the consolations of the scholar in his cave.
I'd go on, but you can see the problem: a question posed
A long time ago, to which different people gave
Such different answers, answers concerning different things.

"What *is* X anyway?" I know the sensible course
Would be to drop those kinds of questions, and just stumble along
Whatever road you'd taken, taking the moments as they come.
Yet some of them have been a part of me for so long—

That race, the picnic at the Institute, the night of the science fair.
Were all those moments the fulfillment of some plan
Or deep attachment, however trivial, or of some abiding care?
Is that what it is—the feeling of a life brought to fruition

On its own terms, whatever terms it chose?
It sounds free, and yet it's rife with opportunities for self-delusion
And bad faith, like the pool of water out of sunlight in the rose-garden,
An epiphany that seems, in retrospect, like a studied illusion.

Was Ariel happy that he'd written all those poems?
He said so, yet beneath them you can almost sense the fear
Of having lived a skeleton's life, in a world of bones.
Perhaps it's best to stay at home and read,

Instead of risking everything for what in the end
Might be of no more significance than a fascinating hobby,
Like collecting bottle caps, or building ships in bottles.
There are smaller choices to be made: hanging about the lobby

Of a hotel vs. watching the Great Downer Avenue Bike Race
From Dave's front porch. Why do we feel the need to create ourselves
Through what we choose, instead of simply sinking without a trace
Into the slow stream of time? The evening light is lovely

On the living room wall, with a gentle touch of green
Reflected from the trees outside. I realize it feels like a letdown
To be told that this is all it comes to—a pleasant apartment
On a shady street a few miles north of downtown,

And yet it isn't all that bad: it offers concrete satisfactions
In lieu of whatever happiness might be; and though I worry that it's
Something I've backed into, at least it's free from the distractions
Of the future, and seems fine for now. As for a deeper kind

Of happiness, if there is such a thing, I'll take a rain check.
We could go shopping for those dishes, try out the new
Pancake House around the corner, or grill something on the deck
And watch a movie. I guess that's what we should do.

THE LATH HOUSE

. . . breathing a small breath.
—Theodore Roethke

1853 (it sounds like a year) First Avenue,
The first house I remember that we lived in as a family.
Oh, there was the bungalow on Maxim Street we rented
While my father was in Korea, where I first discovered dreams,
And before that one in Hollywood I can barely remember,
A few blocks from Grauman's Chinese Theater.
This one had green awnings in the front, a living room
With venetian blinds, a backyard with a garden and a pepper tree,
A small apartment over the garage, and behind all that
An unused lath house filled with dried-out dirt and vegetation,
Where the sunlight filtered weakly through the slats.
There was a shed with windows of translucent Plexiglass
Attached to it in back, with more decaying plants
Amid the spiders and the shadows. I hated going there:
It wasn't frightening so much as claustrophobic and unclear,
Like something difficult to see, then harder to recall.
What I remember most of all are houses, like the large
Victorian manse on Fir Street that I loved to paint
With watercolors, just across the street from where I stayed
When I had chicken pox, with my mother away at work
And my father away again in Japan, with an elderly retired couple—
What *was* their name?—who reminded me of Martha Hoople and the
     Major.

*

I love the way remembering lets the light in, as the sullen gray
Of consciousness dissolves into a yard, a pepper tree, a summer day,
And minor moments and details that had been buried in the past
Take on the clarity of dreams, with a transparency they never had in life.
—It isn't true. Some moments lie beyond the light, like the twins
My sister swears that she remembers when they came home from the
    hospital,
Who lived with us awhile before they died. They're just a blank to me:
It must have been on Maxim Street, and yet there's nothing there.
Sometimes an image of two figures in a crib seems just about to jell,
But it never sets, and then it melts away. I try to see my life
As a single narrative, with parts already there, and others to be filled in
By long chains of association, or the crumbling of a madeleine.
I can't believe that some of them are gone, as if they'd never happened—
Like another person's life, or one that flows in parallel with mine
Along its separate course, made up of the redacted parts
Like the dark matter making up the universe, or the averted face
That slowly turns to you at the climax of a nightmare, as a scream starts.

The neighborhood is gone. Long after we had moved away
There was a fire (I think), and then a freeway through downtown.
Somehow I've saved enough of it to re-create that world,
However incompletely: vacant lots where I caught butterflies
And shot birds with a BB gun whose cocking handle
Smashed my fingers once outside the watercolor house;
The walks home from St. Joseph's in my corduroys and cardigan;
The "Mad Dog! Mad Dog!" chasing me along a wall—
I don't need all of them to know those parts were real. The end
Of Catholic school, the start of physics, track, my father's nervous
    breakdown

All lay in the future. I've gone back to other places where I've lived,
But I can't go there now, which makes it seem the most mysterious of all.
The airplanes coming in for landings at the airport flew so low
That you could see the pilots from the roof, and lying there in the dark
I'd worry that a Russian bomber was descending to destroy us all.
When Nana died I remember listening to my parents murmuring softly
In the early morning darkness as my father packed for Texas
And I wondered if she'd burn in hell because she was a Baptist.
A morbid child? I hope not, though how would I know?
It was all about eternity—a modest one perhaps, but still eternity.
I wish the presence of the everyday could be enough,
The proximity of something small, and breathing a small breath.
It isn't though: it's something incomplete, like a mind half dead to itself
—"You don't *remember* them?"—lingering in the stippled
Shadows of the lath house, in the darkness of the shed behind it.

FEAR OF THE FUTURE

In the end one simply withdraws
From others and time, one's own time,
Becoming an imaginary Everyman
Inhabiting a few rooms, personifying
The urge to tend one's garden,
A character of no strong attachments
Who made nothing happen, and to whom
Nothing ever actually happened—a fictitious
Man whose life was over from the start,
Like a diary or a daybook whose poems
And stories told the same story over
And over again, or no story. The pictures
And paintings hang crooked on the walls,
The limbs beneath the sheets are frail and cold
And morning is an exercise in memory
Of a long failure, and of the years
Mirrored in the face of the immaculate
Child who can't believe he's old.

THE MENOMONEE VALLEY

It was always the first thing Geoff wanted to see
Whenever he'd drive over from Madison to visit me.
He saw it as the quintessential landscape
Of the Essential City, by contrast with that ersatz one

Some eighty miles away, the juvenile capital
Of record stores and gyro joints and bubble gum.
It splits Milwaukee into South and North, the factories,
The bungalows and taverns of the men who used to work in them

Vs. what remains of downtown, the Pfister Hotel, the lakefront
And the mansions of the millionaires who used to own them.
In early spring it's still a nearly frozen wasteland
Of railroad tracks and smokestacks and a narrow, dull canal

Flowing past slag heaps flecked with scraps of snow and seagulls.
Down the road from Badger Bumper, the Miller Compressing Company
Flattens what's left over of the cars, then lifts them up and
Dumps them on a monumental mountain of aluminum and steel,

To be pulverized at last into a kind of coarse, toxic metal meal.
Yet even wastelands change. The noxious smells
That used to permeate the air are gone. The Milwaukee Stockyards
Where we'd stop for lunch (there was a funny restaurant there)

Left town two years ago. The Peck Meat Packing plant
Is rationality itself, with trucks with modern logos and an antiseptic air.
The Tannery, an "Urban Business and Living Center"
Lodged inside the shells of what were once some of the foulest

Factories in the country, is the first stage of a plan
To redefine this "huge forlorn Brownfield" into a different kind of space,
A place of "offices, light manufacturing, a riverfront bike trail"
Meant to ease the lingering traces of a vanishing industrial sublime.

* * *

Geoff moved to California, where he shot himself in 1987.
Growing up in San Diego, I would linger at the list of fifty largest cities
In the *World Book*, San Diego down there near the bottom
And Milwaukee floating somewhere towards the top. The tallest building

Was the EI Cortez Hotel, eight stories high. Lane Field,
Where the Padres played, stood at the foot of Broadway, near the harbor
And the tattoo parlors and the shops purveying cheap civilian clothes.
I remember listening to the Yankees and the Braves in 1958

On my new transistor radio, and dreaming of the day I'd move away—
Which I did when I was seventeen, just before the country
Started changing, before everything I used to take for granted
Started turning into photographs, and to disappear.

You hardly noticed it at first, the demographics shifting
Imperceptibly, the cities on the list displaced by bland southwestern
Sunlight, like the sunlight in Miami at Geoff's funeral.
When I'd go back to visit there were ever taller towers,

Glassed-in skyscrapers that seemed to all be banks.
A freeway turned Pacific Highway into just another throughway
Running past the empty Convair factory, which had closed.
I used to love the seedy section south of Broadway,

With the joke shop next door to the Hollywood Burlesque,
The pawnshops where I'd look at microscopes, and San Diego Hardware,
Where I'd buy materials for the science fair. Like the stockyards,
All that's history now: I heard on NPR last week

The hardware store was moving to the suburbs, driven away
By high rents and a parking shortage in the Gaslamp District, a pathetic
Exercise in urban fantasy designed to recreate a picturesque
Historic neighborhood you think is real, but never actually existed.

* * *

My father's story started in a little town in Texas, Henrietta—
Growing up, then going away to school in Oklahoma,
Juilliard in New York, playing with some orchestras in Europe,
Entering the Navy at the start of WWII, and finally dying of a stroke

About five years ago in San Diego—taken at the end
From Naval Hospital to a quiet hospice overlooking Mission Valley.
It's so much vaster than Menomonee, and yet the moral and the landscape
Seem essentially the same: the minor narratives of individual lives

Played out against a background of relentless change. On my last visit,
Driving down the hill on Texas Street, it seemed to open out
Into a vision of the city of the future: Qualcomm Stadium on the right
And Fashion Valley on the left, and spilling over from its floor

And flowing up the farther side, generic condominiums as far as I could
    see,
Like the ones along the river in Milwaukee. It's as though the dream
Were just to leave those individual lives behind, in all their particularity
And local aspirations, their constraints and disappointments,

For a thin reality that offers fantasies and limitless degrees of freedom—
And for *what*? Sometimes I wonder if it's just finance and entropy,
Although I know that can't be true. Traffic flows in all directions
Through the valleys and across the country, on a grid of possibilities

To be realized in turn, and then abandoned. People move away from home
And die, and the places where they'd lived and whiled away the time
Are temporary, like the units of a mathematical sublime
Reducing what had been a country of localities and neighborhoods

To a bare concept, an abstraction that extends "from sea to shining sea,"
The silence in its fields of derelict machinery and rusting metal
Broken by the din of new construction, as an all-consuming history
Proceeds apace beneath an n-dimensional, indifferent sky.

CLOUDS

I love the insulation of strange cities:
Living in your head, the routines of home
Becoming more and more remote,
Alone and floating through the streets
As through the sky, anonymous and languageless
Here at the epicenter of three wars. Yesterday
I took the S-Bahn into town again
To see the Kiefer in the Neue Nationalgalerie,
A burned-out field with smoke still rising from the furrows
In a landscape scarred with traces of humanity
At its most brutal, and yet for all that, traces of humanity.
What makes the world so frightening? In the end
What terrifies me isn't its brutality, its violent hostility,
But its indifference, like a towering sky of clouds
Filled with the wonder of the absolutely meaningless.
I went back to the Alte Nationalgalerie
For one last look at its enchanting show of clouds—
Constable's and Turner's, Ruskin's clouds and Goethe's
Clouds so faint they're barely clouds at all, just lines.
There was a small glass case that held a panel
Painted by the author of a book I'd read when I was twenty-five—
Adalbert Stifter, *Limestone*—but hadn't thought about in years.
Yet there were Stifter's clouds, a pale yellow sky
Behind some shapes already indistinct (and this was *yesterday*),
As even the most vivid words and hours turn faint,
Turn into memories, and disappear. Is that so frightening?
Evanescence is a way of seeming free, free to disappear

Into the background of the city, of the sky,
Into a vast surround indifferent to these secret lives
That come and go without a second thought
Beyond whatever lingers in some incidental lines,
Hanging for a while in the air like clouds
Almost too faint to see, like Goethe's clouds.

THE ADAGIO

Berlin has a familiar air. It isn't very old
As European cities go, and its amorphous sprawl
Reminds me just a little of Los Angeles—
A place without a single center, offering instead
A set of variations on a theme. With cranes
At its construction sites, graffiti blooming everywhere,
It seems to mask some underlying randomness
Or dream, one whose true significance remains unclear.
Where does the present start, if it isn't in the past?
How should someone set about to live
Within the shadows of another era's history?
These are questions left unasked, or hanging in the air
Above the Reichstag with its glass-and-metal dome
Sitting on the banks of the Spree. I walk its streets alone,
A mind that drifts across the surface of the day
As on a death march starting on the outskirts of the city,
Registering along the way the synagogues and camps,
The churches and the cemeteries, blending them all together
Into one continuous breath, broken up by random
Moments of a private beauty, like the prayers of a devout,
Yet always shadowed by the consciousness of death,
Of beauty's darker underside, as in the filmed reconstruction
Of the conference at Wannsee when, as they're about to leave,
Heydrich puts a piece of Schubert's on the gramophone
And remarks to Eichmann, "The adagio will tear your heart out."

The city feels like that. You start to see connections
Everywhere, as though the fantasy that ended in a bunker

Sixty years ago had happened yesterday—a story
Buried in the morning papers, waiting at the grocery store
As people go about the business of the day. And art is everywhere
As well, and needs its stories too, and if today's seem too banal
Or dull it tries to find them in the air, in fragments
Of that null refrain whose truth lies largely in the telling.
Last week a violinist from the Philharmoniker had dinner here.
She'd settled in Berlin two months ago, and found it . . . well,
"Peculiar," in a word. With culture in the broadest sense
So dominant, and next to nothing to compare it to, it dwells,
She thought, reflexively upon its past, engendering an atmosphere
Of history and the dark whose self-sustaining animus is art.
I think she's mostly right. Sometimes I find myself surprised,
Turning from a book, or looking up to see the sky
Above the tombstones and the family plots at Weissensee,
Or walking down the alleyway that runs along the outer wall
At Sachsenhausen, to realize how fragile all this really is,
How much it draws on memory and the force of the imagination
Just to remain alive. For unless they answered to a need,
The slaughters of the past, along with what was tenderest and true,
Would disappear; unless a shared lament created a reality
Reflecting its own power, making a mythology
Of necessity . . . which may be what the violinist meant.

Spring has come to Wannsee. The ice has melted,
And the ferryboats are floating back and forth again.
It's colder in Milwaukee, and the sky isn't as blue,
But otherwise I think it's basically the same. We try
To tell ourselves that life is local, history is local,
But it isn't true: beneath the details a relentless urge to power
Waits unsleeping for a pretext—like the Reichstag fire,

The falling towers—to let its mindless march resume.
Last night before the reading I was standing on the balcony
Where Max Liebermann, who had the luck to die before the worst,
Watched them marching through the Brandenburger Tor in 1933.
He knew that it was over, that his world was over,
Though nothing *actual* had happened. That lay in the future,
Where the Conference House stood next door to his own.
It was all potential, like a composition waiting to be played.
The music flows so slowly, so inexorably
You hardly notice it at all. Truth is the first to go
—Minor truths at first, then ever greater ones—
Then memory and the personal past, and then the past.
It offers you a way of being free, but then the emptiness sets in—
The freedom of a life without a context, life inside a vacuum
In which none of it had happened, giving up at last
A notice in the newspaper, an announcement on the radio
That someone strains to hear behind the static,
Listening in the distance to the strains of the adagio.

VENETIAN CODA

Sometimes I dream what's called the *male dream*:
I'm going somewhere not too far away, I'm almost there,
When there's a slight delay—a minor detour of no consequence,
But then another, and another, as I get farther and farther
Away from my initial destination, which becomes inaccessible.
Before I left Berlin I went to Venice, a city that reminds me of that dream.
However close you are to where you want to go, the compound
Turnings of its narrow passageways and alleys carry you relentlessly away,
Until you dead-end at a small canal that's nowhere on your map.
The late, wrecked century that started in Berlin, where all roads lead—
I thought I'd find, if not the truth exactly, then at least an inkling
Of some fantasy that lay beneath the placid surface of the day,
The remnants of some dream so many people had to die for. Instead
I watched the boats go by, and clouds traverse the sky
Above an unreal city floating on the water. We're sure at first
That something lies beyond the facts and books, but then we realize it
    isn't there.
Whatever lay behind that slaughter wasn't in the world,
Existing merely in the heart, in memory, in someone's imagination,
Places harboring nothing real. To try to see it is to watch it disappear,
Stranding you a life away from where the unimaginable began,
Staring blankly at your own face floating in the water.

THE DISTINGUISHED THING

Here it is at last, the distinguished thing.
—Henry James

It needn't start with reading
—Though it does—but with an opening
So sweet and self-sustaining that it lasts forever,
A chapter out of all proportion to its years.
Then come those long, perplexing middle parts
I still can't figure out, years that in retrospect
Went by so quickly that I find myself astonished
To see where I am now, on a February day
In my sixty-second year, watching some specks of light
Float before my eyes like small bright snowflakes,
And then disappear. The floating life is next,
An infinite vacation where the days repeat themselves
As in the movie *Groundhog Day*, and time has lost its meaning.
What did they mean, the ones who cautioned us to wait
For all the wishes from the opening to be granted at the end?
Bent over a computer in a study filled with catalogs and magazines,
My life is fine, though not the life I'd wanted or imagined,
For instead of amplitude and progress there's the slow refinement
Of a figure that was there from the beginning, like a pattern in a carpet.
The background is the monochrome from which it sprang,
The null "one color" into which it quietly disappears
On a dull winter day or a warm November afternoon
In a room in sight of the ocean. A life creates a world
That coincides with it, a world in which its narrative unfolds

In all the rich detail that makes it seem so real. It flows from day to day,
Sometimes distracted by the scenery, haunted by the thought
Of something childlike and silent waiting at the end.

The bubble breaks, the figure on the screen dissolves
And leaves me sitting in a comfortable apartment
On a gray midwinter morning more than forty years from home.
I'd read for hours in the brown recliner chair
That sat in my bedroom next to the long row of windows
Giving on the street and canyon and some rudimentary mountains
Hiding an imaginary country that I made believe was home.
I fell for everything those stories said, the stories
Gathered in a Bennett Cerf anthology of "modern fiction"
Hidden in a closet in the hallway with a cookbook
And the *World Book* and *Vogue's Book of Etiquette.*
The leopard's carcass frozen in the snow; the sense of how things are
And how they ought to be, of what's expected or appropriate:
I wonder what I thought those stories *were*—a kind of esoteric knowledge
That would buoy me to the end? It's not that things go wrong
As you grow up, but that they get more complicated, as the certainties
Of seventeen dissolve into the seasons of maturity and doubt—
At least if by "maturity" you mean a sense of resignation,
An indifference to the way your prayers are always answered
When you least expect it, and you've ceased to care.
I felt like I was going home to college when I left,
Caught up in all those fictions of myself time decomposed.
Why do I always think of home as someplace else? Why do I feel,
Each time I go back to New York, a place I've never lived,
That I've returned? All tangled up together at the time,
They seem in retrospect like stages: marriage, Cambridge, moving here

And fatherhood, the shifting cast of friends, the stuff that poems are
   made on
Like the end of marriage and the growing dread of winding up alone,
As one by one your family dies and your career winds down.
It all seems literal and small: the marriage and the moving; the career,
The pension, the prescriptions; the stock banalities of age.
What is that simple truth I want to bring to mind, the truth that lies
   behind
The willful effort to invest these hours with the distant grandeur
Of a different age, and memories that are more about remembering
Than the world they try to re-create? That world is gone,
Supplanted by an unremarkable room where a person sits alone
And tells the story of his life to anyone who's interested, i.e., to no one,
For the others all have stories of their own. That leaves the waiting,
Waiting out the season while the afternoons begin to lengthen
One more time into those beautiful spring evenings, though for what?

There was a sudden lightness as the airplane landed. Ascending, it
seemed that I could look down on my life as though for the first time, and
see that all the possibilities I thought had been closed had been renewed.
The past was as it was, but the future was indefinite, waiting to be filled
with moments distilled from all the moments when I'd been most happy.
I could see us sitting in LaGuardia in 1975, giddy from the weekend out
at Bob's with Doug and Frank, and the evening afterwards at Darragh's,
realizing simultaneously that the time was right for us to have a child. I
could see myself waiting in that same space twelve years later, on a bright
November morning after a dinner with Willy in the upstairs dining room
at Frank's on Fourteenth Street, dumbstruck by the thought that turned
into the last line of the poem I started in to write, "Why do I feel so
happy?" And just twelve years ago, walking along Canal Street on a blue

and blinding February morning, bleary from a wedding that had lasted until two, I felt absurdly happy to be back once more at what still felt like home, walking to my ritual Sunday lunch in Chinatown, then down to a deserted Wall Street, a part of the city I'd somehow never visited before. These moments happened long ago and not so long ago, yet as I gazed at them I realized the happiness that they'd afforded me was still available, still waiting to be experienced again. It was the opposite of the coda of *Swann's Way*, when the narrator, brooding on his own mortality, goes out one morning to a park that had remained for him the locus of an ideal world, dismayed to find that the emotions he'd experienced there had vanished and existed only in his memory, like the carriages and fashions of another age. Instead of wishes, dreams and disappointments, I felt the calm elation of surrendering to the moments, whatever they might hold, that were yet to come, and of not asking for more. Wittgenstein, in the "Lecture on Ethics," spoke of an experience of feeling "absolutely safe," of feeling that nothing could ever injure you, whatever happened, a thought he said was nonsense, though the experience and the feeling are completely real—real as this feeling of life aloft, of drifting day to day across the seasons towards a denouement to be arranged by chance, buoyed by an understanding of the possibilities to come, responding gaily, one fine morning, to obedient hands . . .

—Of course not. It takes a while, or maybe years and years,
But the inevitable eventually arrives, perhaps on a Friday,
Despite some weekend plans, on the way to measure for curtains
Or buy furniture for a new apartment. Time slows down
And words become difficult, as you look around perplexed at where
    you are:

In a too warm room, under sheets that grab, in a gown worn thin and
soft from laundering.
Figures come and go, bringing—what? At times it's dark, at other times
it's light;
Sometimes the dark is broken by a nightlight and the hissing of an
autoclave
Outside the room, or you're abandoned in a hallway, or a room
overlooking a valley
And an ocean you can't see, unconscious of the photographs that
someone must have left.
Why am I so maddened by all this? In the end a life is ordinary, in its
intimate details
And in its underlying themes, including death. I had a vision once,
Which wasn't even mine, of a long breath bounded at its ends by
silence,
Like a sentence following the story of a life until its energy was spent
And its parentheses closed. It's like the childish thought one tries to
overcome,
But never does: that the ending must be true because it seems
mysterious,
As indeed it is, which makes it such a final disappointment—
Like that thought that lingers for a while and disappears, or the vision
That comes to nothing in the end—the nothing that underlies
experience
And until then had been merely an idea, of a distinguished thing.

NORTH CAMBRIDGE

If it was good enough for Eliot to write about,
I guess it's good enough for me, although I only
Lived there for a year, on Dudley Street
At first, across from the trackless trolley yard.
It didn't suit my fantasies at all—the drab apartment
And my two unlikely roommates: Dan,
A counter-counterculture lawyer
Sprung from Harvard and South Boston,
Whom I'd meet most Fridays for a pub crawl
Culminating in dinner, when he'd rise to the occasion
To celebrate "the poor bastard on the bar stool";
And Eric, of indeterminate occupation
And a closet full of magazines of naked boys.
There was a bar on the corner (there was a bar on *every* corner)
Filled each morning with plenty of poor bastards on bar stools
(Night shift from the trolley?) drinking shots and ten-cent beers at 7 a.m.
I had a visit from a friend from college, Ed Kissam,
In town to give a reading for the *Advocate.* Ed's entourage
Consisted of a biker in full leather and a woman with a black beret
Who'd just been raped by rival bikers, which she took in stride.
The president of the *Advocate* wasn't sure just what to make of them,
But endured the evening anyway, and then we all retired—
Ed, the biker, Ms. Beret—to Dudley Street, and called up David Schatz,
My new best-friend-to-be, discovered to live a block away,
Who showed up wearing a purple satin Nehru shirt
À la John Lennon. You can imagine what Dan made of *that*—
Not to mention his house filled with these sixties clowns,

The air of drunken levity, the dope. Things deteriorated after that,
And I departed Dudley Street and moved to David's place
Around the corner on Mass Ave. Fall to winter
And a deepening war: Eugene McCarthy represented hope,
And Johnson gave that speech that left me floored.
Lewis MacAdams and John Godfrey wandered in from Buffalo
In search of the Boston Sound, which didn't actually exist,
Though we discovered "Sister Ray" instead. Winter into spring
And days of wondering what to do about the draft.
John arrived again, and we spent most of spring vacation
Stoned, and wrote a hundred poems—the less said of which
The better—and finally June arrived, and I went back to California
To get married, and in September moved to Porter Square.

All this came rushing back to me at once, and at first
I had no idea why. Then suddenly I remembered
That the spring before I moved to Cambridge
I'd competed in a poetry contest at Mount Holyoke
(John drove me, come to think of it), that in a small way
Saved my life, though that's a story for another day.
There were three distinguished judges, avatars
Of what you wanted to become when you grew up
If genius smiled on you, or you were lucky and persistent.
Last week I got a letter asking me to be a judge
In next year's contest, and I realized the guy who wrote it
Was the same poor soul who'd had to suffer through that evening
At the *Advocate* almost exactly forty years ago.
In my beginning is my end. We poets in our youth . . .
I had a hollow feeling of completion, as though a circle had closed
And I'd become what I'd aspired to—without despondency or madness

To be sure, but without any real satisfaction either, and certainly
Without ever growing up. Do people ever really *change*?
John's a nurse in New York, Lewis lives in California, David in Florida,
All at it in their own ways I suppose. I've no idea where Ed is,
Though I'm sure he's persevering too. Lucky or unlucky,
Bedecked with laurels or languishing in obscurity,
The fact is that we're older, just as time, for all its deceptive
Symmetries, moves in one direction towards one end.
You try to cheat it, finding signs of life, of promises fulfilled,
In what are merely randomness and age, withdrawing from the world
Into a naive dream of art, or of a shared imagination,
But it's never convincing. Sitting on a bar stool in an airport,
Waiting for a flight to take me to a reading, I sometimes
Think that Dan was right in what he meant—that what passes
For ambition and accomplishment is mostly vanity, vanity
And self-indulgence, if not quite in the sense he'd had in mind.
It's all, as Yeats remarked, a silent quarrel with yourself,
One in which internal strife and external equanimity
Cancel each other out, presenting to the world
About the last thing it needs—another modern poet,
One more poor bastard at the wrong end of life.

THIS IS LAGOS

. . . hope would be hope for the wrong thing
—T. S. Eliot

Instead of the usual welcoming sign to greet you
There's the brute statement: *This is Lagos.*
If you make it to the island—if you make your way
Across the bridge and past the floating slums
And sawmills and the steaming garbage dumps, the auto yards
Still burning with spilled fuel and to your final destination
At the end of a long tracking shot, all of it on fire—
You come face-to-face with hell: the pandemonium
Of history's ultimate bazaar, a breathing mass
Whose cells are stalls crammed full of spare parts,
Chains, detergents, DVDs; where a continuous cacophony
Of yells and radios and motorcycles clogs the air.
They arrive from everywhere, attracted by the promise
Of mere possibility, by the longing for a different kind of day
Here in the city of scams, by a hope that quickly comes to nothing.
To some it's a new paradigm, "an announcement of the future"
Where disorder leads to unexpected patterns, unimagined opportunities
That mutate, blossom, and evolve. To others it's the face of despair.
These are the parameters of life, a life doled out in quarters,
In the new, postmodern state of nature: garbage and ground plastic
And no place to shit or sleep; machetes, guns, and emails
Sent around the world from Internet cafes; violence and chaos
And a self-effacing sprawl that simply makes no sense
When seen from ground zero, yet exhibits an abstract beauty
When seen from the air—which is to say, not seen at all.

*

Across the ocean and a century away a culture died.
The facts behind the Crow's whole way of life—the sense
Of who and what they were, their forms of excellence and bravery
And honor—all dissolved, and their hearts "fell to the ground,
And they could not lift them up again. After this nothing happened"
(Plenty Coups), meaning nothing they could do made any sense,
Beyond the fact of biological survival. It's easy to forget
How much of ordinary life, of what we value, long for, and recall—
Ambition, admiration, even poetry—rests on things we take for granted,
And how fragile those things are. "I am trying to live a life I do not
    understand,"
A woman said, when the buffalo and the coups they underwrote were
    gone.
They could have tried to cope. Instead they found their solace
In an indeterminate hope, a hope for a future they couldn't yet imagine,
Where their ways of life might somehow reemerge in forms
Of which they couldn't yet conceive, or even begin to understand.
It was a dream of a different life, a life beyond the reservation
Without any tangible location, predicated on a new idea of the good
With no idea of what it was, or what achieving it might mean—
Like listening to a song with no sound, or drawing an imaginary line
In the imaginary sand in an imaginary world without boundaries.

It feels compelling, and I even think it's true. But these are things
I've only read about in magazines and book reviews, and not
    experienced,
Which was Plato's point—that poets don't know what they talk about.
It doesn't matter though, for most of what we think of as our lives
Is lived in the imagination, like the Crow's inchoate hope, or the fantasies
Of those who leave a village in the country for the city in the smoke.
And when I look in *my* imagination for the future, it isn't hope and
    restoration

That I find but smoldering tires and con men in a world of megacities
And oil fields, where too much has been annexed to be restored.
I have the luxury of an individual life that has its own trajectory and
    scope
When taken on its terms—the terms I chose—however unimportant it
    might seem
From the vantage point of history or the future. What scares me is the
    thought
That in a world that isn't far away this quaint ideal of the personal
Is going to disappear, dissolving in those vast, impersonal calculations
Through which money, the ultimate abstraction, renders each life
    meaningless,
By rendering the forms of life that make it seem significant impossible.
Face me I face you: packed into rooms with concrete beds
And not a trace of privacy, subsisting on contaminated water, luck,
And palm-wine gin, with lungs scarred from the burning air,
These are the urban destitute, the victims of a gospel of prosperity
Untouched by irony or nostalgia—for how can you discover
What you haven't felt, or feel the loss of things you've never known?
I write because I can: talking to myself, composing poems
And wondering what you'll make of them; shoring them
Against the day our minor ways of life have finally disappeared
And we're not even ghosts. Meanwhile life regresses
Towards the future, death by death. You to whom I write,
Or wish that I could write long after my own death,
When it's too late to talk to you about the world you live in,
This is the world you live in: This is Lagos.

NINETY-FIFTH STREET

Words can bang around in your head
Forever, if you let them and you give them room.
I used to love poetry, and mostly I still do,
Though sometimes "I, too, dislike it." There must be
Something real beyond the fiddle and perfunctory
Consolations and the quarrels—as of course
There is, though what it is is difficult to say.
The salt is on the briar rose, the fog is in the fir trees.
I didn't know what it was, and I don't know now,
But it was what I started out to do, and now, a lifetime later,
All I've really done. *The Opening of the Field,*
Roots and Branches, Rivers and Mountains: I sat in my room
Alone, their fragments shored against the ruin or revelation
That was sure to come, breathing in their secret atmosphere,
Repeating them until they almost seemed my own.
We like to think our lives are what they study to become,
And yet so much of life is waiting, waiting on a whim.
So much of what we are is sheer coincidence,
Like a sentence whose significance is retrospective,
Made up out of elementary particles that are in some sense
Simply sounds, like syllables that finally settle into place.
You probably think this is a poem about poetry
(And obviously it is), yet its real subject is time,
For that's what poetry is—a way to live through time
And sometimes, just for a while, to bring it back.

* * *

A paneled dining room in Holder Hall. Stage right, enter twit:
"Mr. Ashbery, I'm your biggest campus fan." We hit it off
And talked about "The Skaters" and my preference for "Clepsydra"
Vs. "Fragment." Later on that night John asked me to a party in New
    York,
And Saturday, after dinner and a panel on the artist's role as *something*
(And a party), driving Lewis's Austin-Healey through the rain
I sealed our friendship with an accident. The party was on Broadway,
An apartment (white of course, with paintings) just downstairs
From Frank O'Hara's, who finally wandered down. I talked to him
A little about *Love Poems (Tentative Title)*, which pleased him,
And quoted a line from "Poem" about the rain, which seemed to please
    him too.
The party ended, John and I went off to Max's, ordered steaks,
And talked about our mothers. All that talking!—poems and paintings,
Parents, all those parties, and the age of manifestos still to come!
I started coming to New York for lunch. We'd meet at *Art News*,
Walk to Fifty-sixth Street to Larre's, a restaurant filled with French
    expatriates,
Have martinis and the prix fixe for $2.50 (!), drink rosé de Provence,
And talk (of course) about Genet and James and words like
    "Coca-Cola."
It was an afternoon in May when John brought up a play
That he and Kenneth Koch and Frank O'Hara—Holy Trinity!
(*Batman* was in vogue)—had started years ago and never finished.
There was a dictator named Edgar and some penicillin,
But that's all I remember. They hadn't actually been together
In years, but planned to finish it that night at John's new apartment
On Ninety-fifth Street, and he said to come by for a drink
Before they ate and got to work. It was a New York dream

Come true: a brownstone floor-through, white and full of paintings
(Naturally), "with a good library and record collection."
John had procured a huge steak, and as I helped him set the table
The doorbell rang and Frank O'Hara, fresh from the museum
And svelte in a houndstooth sports coat entered, followed shortly
By "excitement-prone Kenneth Koch" in somber gray,
And I was one with my immortals. In the small mythologies
We make up out of memories and the flow of time
A few moments remain frozen, though the feel of them is lost,
The feel of talk. It ranged from puns to gossip, always coming back
To poems and poets. Frank was fiercely loyal to young poets
(Joe Ceravolo's name came up I think), and when I mentioned Lewis
In a way that must have sounded catty, he leaped to his defense,
Leaving me to backtrack in embarrassment and have another drink,
Which is what everyone had. I think you see where it was going:
Conversation drifting into dinner, then I stayed for dinner
And everyone forgot about the play, which was never finished
(Though I think I've seen a fragment of it somewhere). I see a table
In a cone of light, but there's no sound except for Kenneth's
Deadpan "Love to see a boy eat" as I speared a piece of steak;
And then the only voice I'm sure I hear is mine,
As those moments that had once seemed singular and clear
Dissolve into a "general mess of imprecision of feeling"
And images, augmented by line breaks. There were phone calls,
Other people arrived, the narrative of the night dissolved,
And finally everyone went home. School and spring wound down.
The semester ended, then the weekend that I wrote about in "Sally's
    Hair"
Arrived and went, and then a late-night cruise around Manhattan for a
    rich friend's

Parents' anniversary bash, followed by an Upper East Side preppie bar
That left me looking for a place to crash, and so I rang John's bell at
    2 a.m.
And failed (thank God) to rouse him, caught a plane to San Diego
The next day, worked at my summer job and worked on poems
And started reading Proust, and got a card one afternoon
From Peter Schjeldahl telling me that Frank O'Hara had been killed.

Ninety-fifth Street soldiered on for several years.
I remember a cocktail party (the symposium of those days),
Followed by dinner just around the corner at Elaine's,
Pre–Woody Allen. It was there I learned of RFK's assassination
When I woke up on the daybed in the living room, and where
John told me getting married would ruin me as a poet
(I don't know why—most of his friends were married), a judgment
He revised when he met Susan and inscribed *The Double Dream of
    Spring*
"If this is all we need fear from spinach, then I don't mind so much"
(Which was probably premature—watering his plants one day
She soaked his landlord, Giorgio Cavallon, dozing in the garden below).
It was where Peter Delacorte late one night recited an entire side
Of a Firesign Theatre album from memory, and set John on *that* path,
To his friends' subsequent dismay, and where he blessed me with his
    extra copy
Of *The Poems*, and next day had second thoughts (though I kept it
    anyway).
Sometimes a vague, amorphous stretch of years assumes a shape,
And then becomes an age, and then a golden age alive with possibilities,
When change was in the air and you could wander through its streets
As though through Florence and the Renaissance. I know it sounds
    ridiculous,

But that's the way life flows: in stages that take form in retrospect,
When all the momentary things that occupy the mind from day to day
Have vanished into time, and something takes their place that wasn't
    there,
A sense of freedom—one that gradually slipped away. The center
Of the conversation moved downtown, the Renaissance gave way to
    mannerism
As the junior faculty took charge, leaving the emeriti alone and out of it
Of course, lying on the fringes, happily awake; but for the rest
The laws proscribing what you couldn't do were clear. I got so tired
Of writing all those New York poems (though by then I'd moved to
    Boston—
To Siena, you might say) that led to nowhere but the next one,
So I started writing poems about whatever moved me: what it's *like*
To be alive within a world that holds no place for you, yet seems so
    beautiful;
The feeling of the future, and its disappointments; the trajectory of a
    life,
That always brought me back to time and memory (I'd finished Proust
    by then),
And brings me back to this. John finally moved downtown himself,
Into a two-story apartment at Twenty-fifth and Tenth, with a spiral
    staircase
Leading to a library, the locus of the incident of Susan, Aladar, and John
And the pitcher of water (I'll draw a veil over it), and Jimmy Schuyler
    sighing
"It's so *beautiful*," as Bernadette Peters sang "Raining in My Heart"
    from *Dames at Sea.*
The poetry still continued—mine and everyone's. I'd added Jimmy
To my pantheon (as you've probably noticed), but the night in nineteen
    sixty-six

Seemed more and more remote: I never saw Kenneth anymore,
And there were new epicenters, with new casts of characters, like
    Madoo,
Bob Dash's garden in Sagaponack, and Bill and Willy's loft in Soho.
John moved again, to Twenty-second Street, and Susan and I moved to
    Milwaukee,
Where our son was born. I stopped coming to New York, and writing
    poems,
For several years, while I tried to dream enough philosophy for tenure.
One afternoon in May I found myself at Ninth and Twenty-second,
And as though on cue two people whom I hadn't seen in years—David
    Kalstone,
Darragh Park—just happened by, and then I took a taxi down to SoHo
To the loft, and then a gallery to hear Joe Brainard read from "I
    Remember,"
Back to John's and out to dinner—as though I'd never been away,
Though it was all too clear I had. Poems were in the air, but theory too,
And members of the thought police department (who must have also
    gotten tenure)
Turned up everywhere, with arguments that poetry was called upon to
    prove.
It mattered, but in a different way, as though it floated free from poems
And wasn't quite the point. I kept on coming back, as I still do.
Half my life was still to come, and yet the rest was mostly personal:
I got divorced, and Willy killed himself, and here I am now, ready to
    retire.
There was an obituary in the *Times* last week for Michael Goldberg,
A painter you'll recall from Frank O'Hara's poems ("Why I Am Not a
    Painter,"
"Ode to Michael Goldberg's (Birth and Other Births)"). I didn't know
    him,

But a few months after the soiree on Ninety-fifth Street I was at a party
In his studio on the Bowery, which was still his studio when he died.
The New York art world demimonde was there, including nearly everyone
Who's turned up in this poem. I remember staring at a guy who
Looked like something from the Black Lagoon, dancing with a gorgeous
Woman half his age. That's *my* New York: an island dream
Of personalities and evenings, nights where poetry was second nature
And their lives flowed through it and around it as it gave them life.
O brave new world (now old) that had such people in't!

* * *

"The tiresome old man is telling us his life story."
I guess I am, but that's what poets do—not always
Quite as obviously as this, and usually more by indirection
And omission, but beneath the poetry lies the singular reality
And unreality of an individual life. I see it as a long
Illuminated tunnel, lined with windows giving on the scenes outside—
A city and a countryside, some dormitory rooms, that night
On Ninety-fifth Street forty years ago. As life goes on
You start to get increasingly distracted by your own reflection
And the darkness gradually becoming visible at the end.
I try not to look too far ahead, but just to stay here—
Quick now, here, now, always—only something pulls me
Back (as they say) to the day, when poems were more like secrets,
With their own vernacular, and you could tell your friends
By who and what they read. And now John's practically become
A national treasure, and whenever I look up I think I see him
Floating in the sky like the Cheshire Cat. I don't know
What to make of it, but it makes me happy—like seeing Kenneth
Just before he died ("I'm going west John, I'm going west")
In his apartment on a side street near Columbia, or remembering

Once again that warm spring night in nineteen sixty-six.
I like to think of them together once again, at the cocktail party
At the end of the mind, where I could blunder in and ruin it one last time.
Meanwhile, on a hillside in the driftless region to the west,
A few miles from the small town where *The Straight Story* ends,
I'm building a house on a meadow, if I'm permitted to return,
Behind a screen of trees above a lower meadow, with some apple trees
In which the fog collects on autumn afternoons, and a vista
Of an upland pasture without heaviness. I see myself
Sitting on the deck and sipping a martini, as I used to at Larre's,
In a future that feels almost like a past I'm positive is there—
But where? I think my life is still all conversation,
Only now it's with myself. I can see it continuing forever,
Even in my absence, as I close the windows and turn off the lights
And it begins to rain. And then we're there together
In the house on the meadow, waiting for whatever's left to come
In what's become the near future—two versions of myself
And of the people that we knew, each one an other
To the other, yet both indelibly there: the twit of twenty
And the aging child of sixty-two, still separate
And searching in the night, listening through the night
To the noise of the rain and memories of rain
And evenings when we'd wander out into the Renaissance,
When I could see you and talk to you and it could still *change*;
And still there in the morning when the rain has stopped,
And the apples are all getting tinted in the cool light.

ROTC Kills

ANALOGIES AND METAPHORS

I want to get out of myself and what I've written,
Yet I wear each moment like a hat. The brim,
The feather stuck in the hatband—what do *they* mean?
What kind of metaphor is *that*? What kind of hat?
I remember an essay I wrote in Luther League
About the soul's journey towards salvation: like a rocket,
I said (it was just after Sputnik), a three-stage rocket
Fueled by discipline and faith (the hydrogen and oxygen)
That roars inexorably aloft until the third stage fires
And the satellite separates and the soul settles into its orbit
Around God, emitting little beeps of praise. "Analogies,"
Said Pastor Paul, "are fine, but never take one to its logical conclusion."

Who needs an MFA when you have Pastor Paul?
I was raised Catholic, then my mother restaged the Reformation
And we all became Lutherans, but I'm indifferent to that now.
What passes for religion in my life is whatever these syllables portend
As your eye moves down the page, following a train of memory and
     thought
To its nonconclusion in a momentary state of mind. All around me
Life pursues the uneventful course that physics sets,
While I navigate another Easter Sunday time and entropy
Are already starting to dissolve—like someone become so immune
To disappointment that it doesn't hurt, for whom salvation lies
In a resistance to reality, in analogies and metaphors that give life shape,
Because the truth is inert. I sometimes used to feel
There was something missing, but I think I'm over that.
The day is wide and meaningless. I doff my hat.

THE RED SHOES

When I was eleven I'd accompany my mother
To San Diego State College, where she was taking courses
For some degree or other (she taught reading to kids).
It was summer. Maybe she didn't want to leave me at home,
Or maybe I wanted to come along—I don't remember.
I was into microscopes and blood: I had a compound model
With three lenses I bought at an optical store on the second floor
Of a Chandleresque building with exposed ironwork,
Like the building in *Double Indemnity*. I would read in the library—
Edgar Allan Poe and *Great Tales of Terror and the Supernatural*,
Where I first read H. P. Lovecraft ("The Rats in the Walls")—
And wander around the Mediterranean-style campus
With its arcades and red tile roofs, overlooking a valley.
One afternoon I came across some people gathered around the corpse
Of a gigantic giraffe sunk in the mud behind the biology building.
It didn't look like something that had once possessed a soul,
But as they did their dissection they let me make a slide of its blood,
Which I stained with a Venetian dye so I could look at its cells
Under my microscope, and compare them to those in birds' blood, and
    my own.
The "Kindly Professor," as I came to call him (he was all of twenty-five),
Let me come to his class and bring my dinky microscope,
Which he showed to his students and deadpanned, "research model,"
As I stood there beaming. The other excitement that summer
Was a movie, *The Red Shoes*, that was showing in a campus theater,
An unlikely choice for a boy of eleven who hated the piano lessons
His father made him take, so I guess my mother made me go.

I sat there in the dark as the Technicolor dream washed over me
And the gorgeous Moira Shearer danced her way to death,
Borne inexorably aloft by the red shoes through the long ballet scene
Towards the oncoming train at the end, when she lay, her body
Broken and bloody, begging Marius Goring, "Take off the red shoes";
And then I walked intact into the sunlight and a cool arcade.

I didn't start out to write a poem about my mother,
But unchecked memories carry you away, like the shoes
In *The Red Shoes*. I'm sure I loved her then:
She was smart and funny and more down to earth
Than my father, who, when he wasn't somewhere with the Navy,
Affected these aesthetic airs and sang too loud in church.
I didn't really mind the trips to the North Park health food store,
Where I'd have a carrot shake, or the pile of pills each morning by my
    millet,
Though they prefigured the manias to come: the single-minded
Ferocity tinged with sweetness, the obsessions with nutrition
And religion, the body and the soul, which led from one fad to the next
Until her heart gave out, and the doctrines dropped away
And she could fill that vacuum with herself. When she was dying
I was stunned to find myself relieved at how unpleasant she'd become,
For it relieved the grief. "When I grow too old to dream /
I'll have you to remember"—I felt my father's sob
As they sang it at the funeral, but then he came into his own
And lived for years and years, his decorating instincts unrestrained at
    last.
I'd visit him each year, and sometimes I'd drive past the college
(Now called a university), which was all new buildings hiding the
    arcades,

The Spanish roofs, the library where I'd whiled the afternoons away
While she went to class, if they're still there at all. The past
Is hidden, but never goes away: I'm spending a semester in the East
And saw that movie yesterday at Film Forum in New York.
(You didn't think that I remembered those two names
After all these years, did you? But the rest is clear as day,
As clear as yesterday.) They're both dead now,
And all I have to wrestle with are words, and yet these
Syllables bring back the feeling of those summer afternoons,
The red tile roofs, the blood and the ballet, as I sit here in the future
I couldn't imagine then, waiting for one I can't imagine now.
Life seems unreal until it suddenly comes back to you,
But by then it's too late—time makes us different people,
Sometimes for better, sometimes, alas, for worse,
But the past is a diversion, and there's nothing you can
Do with it but see it through, and then put it away.
I want to put the memories away, walk out into the cool
Sunlight of a real day, and take off the red shoes.

ALFRED HITCHCOCK

There are four movies that I saw
Between the ages of ten and fourteen that became
Parts of my life, for what that's worth:
The Man Who Knew Too Much, which I saw

When I was ten at the Mission Theatre
On Fifth Avenue, half a block north of the Orpheum.
Doris Day and Jimmy Stewart leave their stylish
London friends completely in the lurch

In their elegant hotel room, and set out in search
Of Ambrose Chapel, which turns out not to be a person,
But rather a church where their kidnapped son is being held.
There's a concert and a clash of cymbals and a shot;

A party at an embassy where she sings "Que Sera,"
While he sneaks up the stairs to find their son.
The suspense becomes unbearable, but it all ends well,
And with their death-defying labors done,

The three of them return at last to their hotel,
Where their friends have fallen fast asleep. *Vertigo*,
Which I'll come back to in a minute, came to the Orpheum
In 1958, followed a year later by *North by Northwest*,

Which is completely captivating—probably the best
Piece of entertainment ever filmed. Cary Grant
Is on the lam, wrongly suspected of an assassination
In a crowded lobby at the United Nations.

He sneaks aboard a train bound for Chicago,
And in the dining car falls in with Eva Marie Saint.
They seem to hit it off, engaging in some quaint
Old-fashioned bantering and flirtation

Before repairing to her sleeping car, where,
Alas, she makes him sleep alone. He has a close call
With a crop duster in a tall cornfield in downstate
Illinois, leaving him covered with dust, yet still impeccable,

And the movie culminates in a scene atop Mt. Rushmore,
Where after clambering around a presidential nostril
Or two he saves her life, and pulls her up into their nuptial bed,
An upper berth back on a train—although the famous phallic finish,

As the train goes roaring through a tunnel, went over my head.
I saw *Psycho* at the California Theatre on Fourth in 1960.
It starts out in a seedy hotel room in Phoenix—so much
Grimmer than the hotel room in *The Man Who Knew Too Much*—

Which foreshadows the seedy Bates Motel. Janet Leigh
Is also on the lam—flight seems to be a reoccurring theme—
And holes up there, and then decides to turn around.
Before she can she's gruesomely dispatched (we later learn)

By Anthony Perkins in the notorious shower scene,
Which tore me out of my seat. He's devoted to his mother,
Who shows up in another scene that made me jump,
As Martin Balsam, a detective fresh from talking to Leigh's lover

John Gavin, heads up the stairs to the mother's bedroom
And she lunges out at him with her brutal knife. She appears again
At the movie's climax, when Leigh's sister, Vera Miles, finds her in the
    fruit cellar
And she slowly turns to her, the way a malignant figure in a dream,

With an averted face, starts to turn to you, and then you scream.
All of these movies were tremendously entertaining, sure,
And a lot of fun, but *Vertigo* was something else again—a pure
Fever dream, a fantasy fulfilled and then at once destroyed.

I saw it again last weekend at the Rosebud Cinema in Wauwatosa,
And it still retains its power to disturb. It's Jimmy Stewart once again,
A wealthy acrophobic retired policeman hired by a college friend,
Tom Helmore, to investigate his wife, supposedly possessed by the ghost

Of her great-grandmother, Carlotta Valdes, who killed herself
At twenty-six, his wife's own age. Kim Novak impersonates the wife
As part of a plot to murder her. Stewart falls in love with her
Of course, but driven forward by Carlotta's furious rage to end her life,

Novak leaps (?) from the bell tower of Mission San Juan Bautista,
Though it's the real wife who falls. Stewart is destroyed. And then his life
Starts to begin again. He meets a shopgirl, Judy (it's Novak again),
And tries to resurrect the past, remaking her in the image of his dead love

Madeleine, until, his fantasy complete, she stands before him in a gauzy
    haze
—And then Carlotta's necklace makes him see the truth. In a daze
He drives her to the mission where the "suicide" occurred,
And struggling against his vertigo he drags her up into the tower

Where—hysterical—she admits to everything. Suddenly a nun
Emerges from the shadows muttering "I heard voices."
Novak screams and plunges to her death. Stewart stands there stunned
And silent, looking down in disbelief at what he's done.

EGGHEADS

In the fifties people who were smart
And looked smart were called eggheads.
Adlai Stevenson, who was bald and went to Princeton,
Was the quintessential egghead, and so he lost
To Dwight Eisenhower, the president of Columbia.
Dave Brubeck was an egghead, with his horn-rimmed
Glasses and all those albums of jazz at colleges,
Though on NPR last week he claimed he wasn't smart.
I took piano lessons from his brother Howard
In the Thearle Music Building in San Diego in the fifties,
Which probably would have made me an egghead by contagion
If it hadn't been for Sputnik, which made being smart
Fashionable for a while (as long as you didn't look smart).
Beatniks weren't eggheads: eggheads were uptight
And buttoned down, wore black shoes instead of sandals,
And didn't play bongo drums or read poetry in coffeehouses.

What sent me on this memory trip was the realization
That stupidity was in style again, in style with a vengeance —
Not that it was ever out of style, or confined to politics
("We need more show and less tell," wrote an editor of *Poetry*
About a poem of mine that he considered too abstract).
The new stupidity doesn't have a name or a characteristic look,
And it's not just in style, it *is* a style, a style of seeing everything as style,
Like Diesel jeans, or glasses and T-shirts, or a way of talking on TV:
Art as style, science as a style, and intelligence as a style too,
Perhaps the egghead style without the smarts. It's politics

Where stupidity and style combine to form the perfect storm,
As a host of stylized, earnest airheads emerge from the greenrooms
Of the Sunday morning talk shows, mouthing talking points
In chorus, playing their parts with panache and glowing with the glow
You get from a fact-free diet, urged on by a diminutive senator
Resembling a small, furious gerbil. If consistency is the hobgoblin
Of little minds, these minds are enormous, like enormous rooms.

It wasn't always like this. Maybe it wasn't much better,
But I used to like politics. I used to like arguing with Paul Arntson
On the Luther League bus, whatever it was we argued about.
It was more like a pastime, since if things were only getting better
Incrementally, at least they weren't steadily getting worse:
Politicians put their heads together when they had to, Fredric March
And Franchot Tone gave their speeches about democracy and shared
    values
In *Seven Days in May* and *Advise and Consent*, and we muddled through.
Everett Dirksen, Jacob Javits, Charles Percy—remember them?
They weren't eggheads or Democrats (let alone beatniks), yet they could
Talk to eggheads and Democrats (I'm not sure about beatniks),
And sometimes even agreed with them. It was such an innocent time,
Even if it didn't seem particularly innocent at the time, yet a time
That sowed the seeds of its own undoing. I used to listen to the radio,
Curious as to what the right was on about now, but I'm not curious
    anymore,
Just apprehensive about the future. I'd rather listen to "Take Five"
Or watch another movie, secure in the remembrance of my own
    complacency,
The complacency of an age that everyone thought would last forever
—As indeed it has, but only in the imagination of a past that feels fainter

And fainter as I write, more and more distant from a bedroom where
    I lie awake
Remembering Sputnik and piano lessons, bongo drums and beatniks,
    quaint
Old-fashioned Republicans and Democrats and those eggheads of yore.

THE GREAT GATSBY

. . . the old island here that flowered once for Dutch
sailors' eyes—a fresh, green breast of the new world.

I've read it dozens of times, starting in high school.
I even listened to it once, on a set of records
I got from the library, sitting in my bedroom by a window
Looking out upon a canyon and a mountain to the east.
The earnest interplay of sentiments and sentences
Propels you forward, past the parties and the beautiful shirts,
The lists, the midtown brightness, towards the moonlight
And the green light and the water waiting for you at the end.
It's like the record of a dream, compelled in equal parts
By personality and history, by public destiny and geography
Played out in private, that each time I'd pretend to share.
I hate comparisons: a thing should be unique, and fill its space.
And yet there's something irresistible about what isn't there,
The beckoning undefined that cloaks itself in metaphors,
The *something else* that waits to take the place of what you have.
It holds the promise of a better life, or at least a different one,
And so I started on my quest, a voyage centered vaguely
On Manhattan, and whatever else that might turn out to mean.
My ticket was an aptitude for SATs. My *Half Moon*
Was a Greyhound bus that found a passage to the East.

The things you seek are never those you find. As one
Supplants the other each remains unreal and unexplored,
And yet the bare geography is still the same. The passage west

Became a fresh, terrestrial paradise, and then a state of mind,
Though on the ordinary maps they coincide—the meadows
That were Harlem, and the forests that became Times Square;
The place where Sneden's Landing turned into a song.
What started out as commerce gradually became the old idea
Of a new form of grace, a prolonged "capacity for wonder,"
Then for something harder to define. The commercial venture
Petered out somewhere near Albany. The space it opened up
Stayed open through the four succeeding centuries, altered
Into something no one on the ship could even recognize.
The next voyage failed too. The Northwest Passage
Was a myth, though an essential one, a kind of catalyst.
The ship of state "had somewhere to get to and sailed calmly on"
—Distracted now and then by revisions and upheavals—
Towards a mysterious destination that continues to recede,
While Hudson and his son and a remnant of his crew,
Set adrift in a small boat, vanished from history.

Sometimes I wonder what I'm doing here, in a reduced
Midwest, amid what's left of the "thrilling returning
Trains" of the Milwaukee Road, listening to Mabel Mercer
Singing "Did You Ever Cross Over to Sneden's?"
And reading *Gatsby* one more time. What I had in mind
When I set out from San Diego on that bus had as much to do
With the real world as Tomorrowland did with the real future,
Which is where I find myself today. In the art museum's basement
There's a Thomas Cole landscape of a mountain in a storm,
Ablaze in the imaginary wilderness that ended centuries before.
What starts in wonder and a promise settles into a hope
That springs eternal, and then into disappointment, as the end

Becomes so grandiose and undefined there's nothing there to see.
That's the trouble with the sublime: it feels so full of purpose
At the outset, yet as time goes by it comes to seem beside the point,
Like a dream I'd only wished I had. Who cares if it came true—
And even if it did, how would I know? I'd have felt the same,
No matter what I'd started out to do, and in any case, as Gatsby said,
It was just personal. And when I try to think of what it meant,
I can't remember—it was all so long ago, and it was new.

THE WHOLE CREATION

FOR HAROLD BLOOM

I still believe in it, though I don't know who else does.
I first experienced it in the building I have an office in now
And called it poetry, but the word was just a placeholder
For something undefined, though that's too simple a way to put it.
You aspire to what you admire, whether you understand it
Or not, and now that I've retired into it, I want to remain here
In my home away from home, roaming without sadness
Through the whole creation, through the long song of myself.
Some days I wake up in a room suffused with sunlight
"Like a yellow jelly bean," as Jimmy Schuyler put it
In his great poem "Hymn to Life," but it's not that kind of day.
There was a blizzard overnight, and everything's shut down,
Including my seminar, and so instead of ruminating on that poem
I'm fooling around with this one, and looking out the window at the snow.
What *is* poetry anyway? It falls like snow, and settles where it falls,
And melts. I thought I was going to wake up in another world,
And so I have, but it's the one where I began. The sunlight
Just came back, as what begins in gladness and uncertainty matures
Into a kind of baffled happiness, unfinished and complete.
I have the sense of something constantly receding, the way
The future does, then suddenly returning, like the past.
It's all so confusing, and yet it doesn't bother me—
Everything evaporates, but some of it eventually comes back
In the uncertain form it assumed in the first place—
A remnant still intact and seemingly as distant from me
As the books in the library I keep remembering and looking up,
And as close as them too. But I loved it, whatever it was.

ROTC KILLS

FOR FABRIZIO MONDADORI

I'm retired, I'm sitting in a house I made
In my imagination years ago, that now is real.
On the walls are posters from the Harvard
Strike in 1969 I saved for their designs
And then forgot about, and now they're here:
STOP HARVARD EXPANSION, STRIKE
FOR THE 8 DEMANDS, and then the best of all,
In tiny red letters with three red bayonets,
rotc kills (pronounced *rot-cee kills*). From here inside
Time seems unreal, I'm back in graduate school,
But then the mind ascends and time becomes objective,
I'm myself again, at home again, and sixty-four.
The particulars of a life, the pattern of a life:
These are the poles the mind, in the guise of a poem,
Floats back and forth between. The calm elation,
The deflating sigh: the trees are tossing in the wind, the leaves
Unfurl their silvery undersides, the soft clouds drift across the sky.
Time may be an abstraction, but it makes the days go by,
The days I never thought I'd see, when the music of the sixties
Lost its way, became too faint to hear, the voices fell away,
And then it all came down to *me*. What *were* those eight demands?
I can't recall to save my life. I lived there, I breathed that air,
And sometimes some of it drifts back to me. "You should join PL,"
Paul said as we were sitting in the lounge. Picketing
The GE plant in Lynn didn't much appeal to me, so I just

Said it seemed too hard to square with being married
And finishing my degree. "Yes! That's what's so great about it!"
He replied, as I rolled my eyes. Or Jonny Supak's plan
To hold the chairman (Rogers Albritton) hostage in his office:
"The kids are stealing underwear from Filene's Basement,
Asking for the Red Army! 'Where's the Red Army?' they're asking!"
It felt so all-important at the time, in a surreal way, the endless
Back-and-forths, the forums, teach-ins, meetings and analyses, strategic
Planning sessions ("But—but that would be *capitulationism!*"),
And look at what it came to. I didn't even vote in 1968
(Chicago was too fresh), but on election night I found myself
Nostalgic for the Hump, only by then it was too late.
It's nice to think it might have made a difference,
But that's just wishful thinking: money finds a way,
And if it wasn't Nixon . . . Too much has gone
To be restored, and as for money = speech, it's a joke:
The silence in what people used to call the streets
Is deafening, all talk is on the radio, as money
Quietly wraps its hands around the country's throat.

I wonder what Larry, my general contractor, Jeff,
My carpenter, Jerry, who (occasionally) did the plumbing,
Made of all the posters. They couldn't be more friendly,
But Wisconsin's a peculiar state—La Follettes vs.
Tail-Gunner Joe, the sewer socialist mayors of Milwaukee
And the park where Hitler lovers rallied. I'm not sure
I could explain them in a way they'd understand
("See, there were these demands"), but then there's Mitch,
The landscape guy, whose countercultural compulsion to explain
Is straight from Paul and Jonny. It's beautiful out here,

I feel alive and out of it, from the aisles of the Piggly Wiggly,
The World of Variety, to the steps of the Unique Cafe,
The shelves of Gasser Hardware. Driving through "the vast
Obscurity beyond the city," it suddenly seems so clear,
Though the clarity is probably deceptive, as clarity often is:
Beyond the signs for prefab homes (I bought one),
Pro-life billboards with a baby floating in what looks like
Amniotic fluid ("Before I formed you in the womb I knew you"),
Madmen on the radio denouncing Baptists and Freemasons,
Lie the streams, the rivers, the steep, unglaciated hills.
You couldn't climb them (would you want to?),
But it's comforting to know they're there. We live in different
Dreamworlds, wandering through a wilderness of words,
While the real story writes itself in silence. It's forty years ago,
It's yesterday, and when I try to think of what those posters represent
I realize they're footnotes, surface irritants that left the underlying
Language undisturbed. Their meaning is the interval between the times
Of then and now, the times of looking forward and of drifting back.
"They flash upon that inward eye," and then they're gone,
I'm sitting in a room, I'm looking at the trees, unsure if this is
Something other than another version of *The Big Chill*,
A movie I despise. I hope it is. I saw Paul not too long ago—
He's mellowed, everyone has mellowed, "mellow"
Is a word for disappointed. The sixties had their charms
But patience and contentment weren't among them.
It was a brief, imaginary time, swept along by anthems
And guitar heroes, when tomorrow had arrived,
The air was filled with specious possibilities,
All the demands were just, the kids kept calling
For the Red Army, and rotc killed.

LIKE GODS

The philosopher David Lewis spun a fantasy of two omniscient gods who know about one world, which might as well be ours. Each knows precisely all there is to know, the grand "totality of facts, not things." Each knows the pattern of the light on each neglected leaf millennia ago. Each knows the number of the stars, their ages, all the distances between them, all the "things too tiny to be remembered in recorded history—the backfiring of a bus in a Paris street in 1932," as well as all the things that history distorts or just can't see, like·the thought that must have flashed across Patroklos's mind (if he'd existed and had had a mind—the middle knowledge of the schoolmen) when Hektor split his stomach with a spear (if he'd existed too). Each one looks on, as though through ordinary eyes, as "Mme Swann's enormous coachman, supervised by a groom no bigger than his fist and as infantile as St. George, endeavoured to curb the ardour of the quivering steel-tipped pinions with which they thundered over the ground," and sees "the grey 'toppers' of old" the gentlemen strolling with her wore, the little "woollen cap from which stuck out two bladelike partridge feathers" that she wore (or would have worn if they and she'd been real). Each monitors the photons through the slits, the slow decay of radium, and knows the ratio of vermouth to gin in someone's first martini at Larre's. Each knows what Darragh, Geoff, and Willy knew before the bullet or the pavement killed their worlds, and where the shots came from in Dallas. Each knows precisely what the other knows, in all the senses of those words, and if a question has a factual answer, each can answer it. Yet there's a question neither can resolve: Which god am I?

The question posits both a world and a unique perspective on that world, which neither has. And if gods One and Two could reify themselves by wondering who or what they were, they'd have to know the answer—and, because they don't, they can't. Could gods like those be real, in something like the sense that you and I are real? But then, what sense is that? Gods One and Two are you and I writ large: I wander out into the day and feel the sunlight on my face. I see the sunlight on the first spring leaves like green foam on the trees, and so do you. The world we have in common, that the gods can comprehend in its entirety, remains beyond my grasp, and yours. The world I know belongs entirely to me, as yours belongs entirely to you. I know my world completely, as the gods know ours, because it's nothing but my take on things, and starts and ends with me. I'm both the author and the captive of my world, because my take on things is all there is to me. When Mary, in Frank Jackson's philosophical diversion, wanders from her room of black and white and shades of gray and finally sees a rose, and then goes on in sunlight, into the Hofgarten, and drinks coffee, and talks for hours, it's hard to see how all of *this* (as she might say) could be an artifact of her perspective. But it is.

So what? Philosophers tell stories, but they make them up, and what are they to me? Sometimes I think I'm humoring myself (a good thing I suppose) with an extended exercise in nonsense. *Have breakfast, have a cup of strong black common sense, get over it,* I tell myself, refuting Berkeley with my foot. Instead of this entanglement of self with self, why can't I just relax into my place inside the natural order, be a thing within the solid scheme of things, a Dane in Denmark? How can fantasies, unreal by definition, show me what I am, and know? How can the poetry of possibilities dissolve the prose of facts? My little life sustains me while it can, and that's enough. It may be all contingent, but it's real, and when catastrophes occur, as they inevitably do, I'd rather they occur to *me,* instead of writing them away, or redefining happiness or sorrow or tranquillity as alterations of some abstract point of view that points at nothing. Inescapable illusions must be real, or might as well be real, no matter where reflection on them leads; and if accepting them means taking things on faith, that's fine. Who wants to be a posit, or a site of possibilities? Who wants to walk out and evaporate into this green spring day? Who wants to have sex with a wraith?

No matter where reflection on them leads. It leads, of course, to me. A cri de coeur is not an argument, but where the real argument begins. Hopkins: "searching nature I taste *self* but at one tankard, that of my own being." Kant: "a feeling of an existence without the least concept," meaning that despite the certainty I have, I've no idea what I really am, or where, and as for "searching nature," I have no idea even where to start. These matters mean the world to me, and yet no matter how I try to come to grips with them, they slip away. *I* and *here* and *now* are ever present, yet they vanish in the act of apprehension, as a poem turns into language as you write it down. Dimensionless, atemporal, imprisoned in the present—even as I say them to myself the words fall short of what I thought I started out to say, like the conclusion of an argument too close to me to share, or like an empty thought-balloon that hangs above me in the air. It's not the question of what makes me who I am through time—of how a figure in a photograph from 1985, a couple sitting in the garden of the small Hotel des Marronniers just off the rue Jacob, could be the person who remembers her and thinks of him today—but of what constitutes me now, and of what made me then. If giving it a name won't help, then neither will pretending it's divine. If I should be supplanted by a bright recording angel knowing everything about me in the way the gods know all about their world, I wouldn't have survived. She takes the whole thing in—the house on Maxim Street, the bike rides down the hill on Wabash Street, my high school friends, their friends, the friends of friends of friends—with eyes that monitor my back, my face, the traces in my brain projected on a screen, the n degrees of separation linking me to nearly everyone who's ever lived, a thing within a wilderness of things, with each one locked inside a universe with no outside, of which there's nothing she can see. How could it be an afterlife? It's just a different life, another life, complete or incomplete as anyone's, consumed by questions that elude it, not because she can't remember, but because the words that make them up are undefined: Which one of them was I? Which world was mine?

SELF-PORTRAIT ON YOUTUBE

His reasoning was specious, and did much to reassure me.
—P. G. Wodehouse

Like a casement opening out upon a world
He chooses not to see, the prisoner of a point of view
Remains complacent in that choice, until a slight
Alteration of perspective, a trick of light, reveals a small
Illuminated window in a corner of the factory's dull facade.
I don't like looking at myself (*I like to watch myself,*
Says the countervoice)—how can that odd, uncomprehending
Object looming right in front of me be *me (and there I am)?*
I was wandering through the Internet last week
(As if I'd nothing better to do) in a dilatory state of mind,
Revisiting my usual sites, checking my email now and then
For news of something interesting or new or strange,
And then I came across myself. I was standing at a podium
In a bookstore, reciting a poem I wrote last summer
About the sixties, about how the world you believed you knew
Changes in ways you couldn't have foreseen; about disappointment.
It all seemed tentative, yet tentative in a way I wanted it to be,
For thought itself is tentative. As the reader plodded along
A sense of peace came over me, as though the person I was watching
Were the real me, relieved of the burdens of self-consciousness
And spelling out the words as I had meant them all along. Perhaps
Life *is* best looked at from a single window (I saw *Gatz* last week too,
Another objectification of self-consciousness, of perfect sentences),
But a perspective boxes you in. To see yourself the way others see you

Is a wonderful kind of freedom, the freedom of starting over again
Without preconceptions, the freedom of looking at your heart.
I'm at the age when death becomes a fact, however long deferred,
Instead of just an abstract possibility, which is why I crave distractions.
The mirror is too intimate. What I want is the cool detachment
Of another person's vantage point, free from the distorting
Self-conceptions consciousness imposes on itself, when the mind
Is caught in the brief interval between thought and action
And it finds a way of moving forward, and it's time to start.

THE EMERGENCE OF THE HUMAN

You can watch it as you walk through the Uffizi:
Gold leaf, egg tempera, gold halos on the flat saints
And on the flat Madonna and detached bambino
Balanced precariously on her lap, her eyes to one side.
The composition is meant to look like something you can't see,
To illuminate a mystery. Yet now and then some vaguely
Contoured hills replace the gold, a figure seems to look at you
Or look like someone from the artist's town, or the baby's
Features soften into the faint suggestion of a smile.
The impulse is always towards the truth, the only question is
The kind of truth: iconic or demystified, a representation of the word
Or the word made flesh. Siena's figures floated on the surface,
Shorn of their misgivings and desires, while somewhere down the road
Something was happening of which Siena didn't have a clue.
You can see it happen in the landscapes in the background,
Drifting from nowhere in particular into those bluish
Mountains harboring the caves I saw last week; in Christ's
Contorted features made of paint that feels like flesh,
That yields a massive Holy Family without halos;
In the reinvention of mythology, and then within mythology,
The shift from Venus chaste and balanced in the foam,
Caressed by winds, to Venus lying on a bed with a small dog at her feet,
A "nude woman" who stares at you indifferently and reeks of sex.
And then the floodgates open and the world comes rushing in:
The "crude, expressive naturalism" of Caravaggio and his followers—
Medusa on a shield, screaming from her mouth's black hole,
And then a real Cardinal, palpably corrupt, and Bacchus

As a smirking peasant boy, his upper body glistening with sweat,
And then a blood-soaked dental scene of overwhelming cruelty, then
    a thug;
All hanging in an exhibition in the Pitti Palace just across the bridge.
"And I am sweating a lot by now" as I make my way along Via Romana,
Following this trajectory—a trajectory that started with a mystery
And peeled away its layers to reveal the human form inside—
To its logical conclusion in La Specola, the anatomical museum
Filled with specimens of almost every living thing,
And then the finally human body, open for the world to see,
Like David flayed, or St. Sebastian disemboweled
Instead of punctured here and there by arrows, and brains
Where golden halos used to be. Somewhere in the remote past
There was a message from an angel. What happened next
Depends on whom you ask, but if you ask me, I'd say it led to these—
These wax models of the body, with its veins, entrails, and nerves,
From which nothing is missing except its old significance;
As though the history of art were the story of its disappearance,
Of the deflation of the word into a slowly disappearing
Word made flesh, of the flesh demystified at last.

1135

No one has to write any special way—
You make it up as you go along. I started
Writing this way—no thoughts at first,
Then a lot of words in the guise of thoughts,
Then real thoughts—a long time ago.
You can write or think about death directly,
Or you can write about it by indirection
And delay, the way the diary of a day
Reflects the silence waiting darkly at the end,
Like the silence lingering after graduation,
When the students have all gone away
And the ghost campus descends.
I don't know what to say about Darragh—
A painter who gradually convinced himself
That he saw what he didn't actually see,
Until finally he couldn't see at all. I loved him
In a way, though the "in a way" tells all:
There was something not quite there, and now
There's nothing there at all. I drove by his house
Last Saturday, when I was visiting Bob.
Vines and weeds were everywhere, bushes
Encroached upon the porch, there was a dull,
Uneasy feeling something bad had happened there
That left an empty house with empty windows
I had to stretch to see through, staring into rooms as
Empty as a skull from which the mind has gone.
I couldn't look in the studio. I took pictures

Of the For Sale sign, and then drove home
Or what felt like home. The Saturday afternoon
Was bland and beautiful, with no sense of an ending
Or the thought that gradually insinuates itself
In the back of the mind, in a studio, alone.

WATCHFUL WAITING

Let's see what happens.

I'm waiting at the bar at Gene's, a place
On West Eleventh Street, just down the street
From the Larchmont Hotel, where I usually stay
When I'm in New York. I come to New York a lot
Since I've retired (from what? someone asked).
Gene's is down some stairs, and sitting at the bar
You can watch people walking by through a window
Above your head, the way I'd imagined New York
When I was a kid, or imagine Dawn Powell's New York.
I sometimes think of life as a vicarious attempt
To make sense of yourself, balancing what you did
And didn't do so that they'll come out even at the end;
And then I think that's probably a waste of time.
It's not a book at all: there's too much time,
And then it's gone; that sense of something waiting
To unfold is missing, leaving only the waiting,
And when something does occur it's always late,
Too late and incomplete, like a small residue of feeling.
We care too much about feelings—feelings for what?
Feelings can be stupid, maybe not in themselves,
But in the way they magnify and reduce, leaving you
Exhilarated and confused. I guess I'll call Diane
In a while, to see what I have to say. I could tell her
About the things I saw today: the anti-Kitty show
At the Japan Society; Shio Kusaka's white pots

With small blue dots; the drawings at the Morgan;
Eataly and Shake Shack; these people in the window
Walking by on their way home, or God knows where.

That's the thing about time: it can take you anywhere,
And yet it takes you home. It leaves you the same person
In a different place, still always metaphysically alone,
But with friends that you can phone and tell your travels to.
I can't tell you what it is, but I can feel it flow, and flow away,
Until a memory breaks its spell and I'm in school again,
Or on a bus to college, or walking down Fifth Avenue in a daze.
The memory doesn't matter—what matters is the interval
It restores to life, the feeling of abstracted time made tangible,
Of duration without any destination, of a sense of a life.
I keep reading my story over and over again, my one story.
"Readers of this column are probably familiar with its details"
And I won't go over them again—they're as changeless
As the pages of those novels I keep rereading on the planes
To New York, washed in a noir California light, the scent
Of canyons after rain, the house on a canyon I won't see again.
Does it make any difference? I try to tell you these things
Not out of an urge to communicate—you have your stories too—
But for their own sake, and my sake too, and to make the days go by,
As though the point of taking stock were just to pass the time
Until there isn't any more, and the art of losing were its own reward.
Is that really the best one can do? To stay at home forever, living,
As Wittgenstein once put it, entirely in the present, burnishing the words
Until they're like a second nature, better than the first one, as though
Living in the moment weren't to simply let life happen, but to get it right?
Why is everything "as though," that great hope of the subjunctive life?

I ought to decide where I'm going to eat tonight. In *Hebdomeros*,
Giorgio de Chirico's novel in the form of an extended thought,
There's a passage about "those men who eat alone in restaurants,"
Inhabiting "the infinite tenderness, the ineffable melancholy"
Of a moment "so gentle and so poignant that one doesn't understand
Why all the personnel of the premises, the manager and cashier,
The furniture, the tablecloths, the wine jugs, down to the saltcellars
And the smallest objects don't dissolve in an endless flood of tears."
I think there's so much freedom in that thought: you stroll out
Into the night as (!) into a wilderness of traffic lights and neon signs.
I love feeling lost in the Village: crossing Seventh Avenue
Below West Tenth I get confused, and I love feeling confused,
Like a lamb in "The Whiffenpoof Song"—following the confusion
Wherever it may lead and (as I said a page ago) exhilarated too.
Later I can find my way back home ("wherever that may be"),
But now I'm wandering through a maze whose every prospect pleases,
Lingering on the curbs and corners as I make my way to nowhere
In particular, celebrating the end of the day with a drink and dinner
And a slow walk back to my hotel, pausing to look at the menu
Of a new restaurant at the end of Greenwich Avenue, across from
Mxyplyzyk, in the space where Café de Bruxelles used to be.

"Watchful waiting" is a way of handling prostate cancer.
It's such a gradual disease that rather than immediately rush in
With scalpels or radioactive seeds, you take a wait-and-see approach,
Ready for the worst if it should come to that, but meanwhile
Letting nature take its course. The worst is always on your mind
Of course, but at least it's not a foregone conclusion, as it is
With so many other cancers: browsing a famous blog last week
(A blog where poets seem to go to die), I saw that Paul Violi had died.

I'd always liked him, though I hadn't known him well. In January
He was diagnosed with pancreatic cancer; ten weeks later he was dead.
It made me think of David Sachs, a philosopher and boyhood friend
Of my advisor Rogers Albritton (emphysema). He'd had his heart set
On retiring to Scandinavia, but as retirement approached was diagnosed
With pancreatic cancer too, and died. It "concentrates the mind,"
As Samuel Johnson said of hanging, but what it concentrates mine on
Isn't the past I usually brood about, but the idea of the future—
Not the political future, which I've given up on, but the personal
Future, with its fragile possibilities and plans. Starting from the past
You move along a settled arc of life that leads from then to now;
But since the future isn't fixed the road that leads you on from there
Is open-ended, like starting out in the evening without any end in view.
The journey, not the distant destination; the scenes along the way,
And not the long look back—all great advice I guess, if great advice
Is what you want, instead of simply waiting for a shoe to drop.
Hello, Diane. I don't even know where I'm calling from anymore,
Because the scenery keeps changing: I'm wandering around New York,
And then I'm back in San Diego on a canyon, or I'm sitting on the
Deck at the Bean House, or at the Wright House in Two Rivers,
Looking at the view across the river as the fog rolls in and the light
Keeps changing, and the only constant is unchanging change.
"Unchanging change": that phrase is from "The Crystal Lithium,"
A poem of Jimmy Schuyler's I adore—his great long poems remain in
Place as they move forward, marking their time until there isn't anymore.
I know that I'm repeating myself, yet it's precisely what I want to do:
There's a kind of naturalness and grace that comes with repetition,
With advancing by accretion through a space of rediscovered possibilities
Into a new world, which is the old world once removed, where I can
Almost imagine your face, and my face too, you to whom I write

Without writing, as though in talking to myself I also talked to you.
We both know life is an adventure. Death is an adventure too,
Like an experiment to be concluded in the laboratory of the future,
One whose outcome is completely certain, yet impossible to observe.
The suspense is in the details, as it morphs from an abstraction
Into something personal and real, drifting from the dark shadows
At the back of the mind into the bland light of an ordinary day.
And just as the fear of death and the unknown becomes diminished
By coming out into the open, so life accommodates its end
By starting over, by leaving home to find another place to live.
Where was I, and where am I now? I know of course
Exactly where I am—at the desk in my study in Milwaukee—
But that's beside the point. It's where you are in your imagination
That's important, for the life of simply staying where you are
Is a shadow's life, that leaves you by yourself, alone and scared.
Why can't we just move on? The light up ahead is soft
And seems to beckon us, glowing with a promise of beginning
Once again, as if there were still time. Do you remember
The "death march" along Via Veneto, and the Big Happy Bed
In Berlin? I don't think of them as memories, but as opportunities
To take advantage of or miss. Why don't we both revisit them,
Not to try to bring about the past, which was Gatsby's fallacy, but as part
Of what the future holds in store, where there might even be room
For that dog (although I can't imagine where)? Even Gene's,
Where all of this began, keeps pleading with us to appear once more
In the window over the bar and amble down the stairs. There's so much
Left to do, and redo, before it's time for me to show up on that blog—
The question is if we should make it new, or try to get it right,
Or put the question to one side and stroll once more into the night,
Or onto crazyJet and fly to Paris from Berlin, and check into

That terrible hotel, La Louisiane, the one you nicknamed
Hotel Claustrophobia, and make our way along the rue de Seine
To the Metro out to La Défense, then back to the hotel and to a night of
Quiet bickering over dinner at Allard. We could go there again
And stay in a better hotel, or just be less fastidious this time around;
Or we could visit someplace new. I've always wanted to go
To Mexico, though perhaps this isn't a propitious time. Anyway,
At least it sounds like a kind of plan, however vague. Shit,
We could go to Vegas.
                    C'mon, Diane!

The Swimmer

THE ARROGANCE OF PHYSICS

The twentieth century was the century of physics:
The physical world came close to being tamed
By understanding, making it harder to understand
Or even imagine, on the scale of the cosmos
And on the order of the very small: time passes
As your twin ages, while you remain perpetually young—
Though a lot of good it does you, existing as you do
At no place in particular, smeared out everywhere
Until someone sees you and your wave packet collapses.

It was also the century of poetry, modern poetry
And the question it engendered, which it keeps repeating:
"Are you just going to go on writing poems like this,
Writing for posterity? Posterity isn't interested
Unless you are, because instead of a quaint immortality,
It offers merely intermittent moments of attention
Before moving on, maybe to return, but probably not.
You can't displace your heroes in the pantheon,
Because there isn't one: just this giant, happy band
Of suppliants, each one knowing what the others know.
I realize this isn't what you'd hoped for, but please,
Don't get discouraged—celebrate temporality instead."

So here I am, sitting in a park thirty years after writing
"In the Park," a poem I'd hoped might last forever.
They finally discovered the Higgs boson, which means that
Physics is still on track, though no one knows to where.

I still believe in it, of course, though it's so removed
From everything I think I think there's nothing to imagine
Beyond equations, which is fine—it was equations all the way,
Until I came to poetry and knew that it was what I had to do.
And now look where I am, what I've become: a marginal observer
Of a universe of my own devising, waiting on a denouement that never
    comes,
But that continues through an afternoon that's wider than the sky, whose
Mild, unearthly blue conceals an emptiness resounding like a gong
Tolling for no one, while I sit here in the safety of my song. Like the
    hedgehog,
I still know what I know, although it matters not at all: I labor over it,
And yet it's written in a different idiom, full of sound and fury,
Signifying—what? It can't be nothing, though it might as well be
If it can't be rendered in the language of the stars. I want to
Speak to something far away, beyond the confines of the page,
But it won't listen, and to everything I say it answers No.

VON FREEMAN

I was a rock-and-roll child. I saw Elvis
Truncated by Ed Sullivan, listened to Fats Domino
Sing "Blueberry Hill" and loved "Sixteen Tons,"
Which was proto–rock and roll. I still love it,
But since you can't remain a child forever,
I cast my net wider, and thanks to my Japanese
Integrated amp, saxophones wash over me each night.
It started with Paul Desmond, who aspired to sound
"Like a dry martini," and went on to bring to life
The celebrated and obscure alike: Spike Robinson,
Whom I heard at the Jazz Estate a few blocks away
In 1992; Frank Morgan, who had Milwaukee ties
And whom I wanted to nominate for an honorary degree,
A scam set up for local businessmen; and Coltrane
Of course, that endless aural rope that curls upon itself
And then uncoils. And it wasn't simply saxophones: Chet
Baker's trumpet, plangent and permanent as he fell from
Young and beautiful to wrecked and toothless; and Bill Evans,
Still perfecting "Autumn Leaves" at Top of the Gate,
While downstairs in the streets the '60s boiled. Von Freeman
Died last week at 88. I hadn't heard of him until he died,
And now here he is, filling up my room with "Time After Time."
He believed in roughness, and on leaving imperfections in
So his songs wouldn't lose their souls, which is how I think of poems.
Philip Larkin loved jazz too—a great poet, though disagreeable—
But I don't know if other poets on my radar do. Maybe they
Think it's easy, I say to myself as I put on a record of Mal Waldron's,
To whom Billie Holiday once whispered a song along a keyboard
In the 5 Spot and Frank O'Hara and everyone stopped breathing.

MISS HEATON

She was probably younger than I remember her—
A small, white-haired lady who taught Honors English
To twelfth-graders. I was sixteen, completely gone
On math and physics, though I had an "amateur" interest
In modern literature, the more advanced the better,
Which was probably due to mathematics: Faulkner, Joyce,
Virginia Woolf, wherever the stream of consciousness meandered.
She disapproved: "Why don't you read some Thomas Hardy?"
She suggested while I was working on an Advanced Placement
Essay on "Daffodils" or "Stopping by Woods on a Snowy Evening"
(I don't remember which). Eight years ago someone who
Likes my poetry emailed "Proud Songsters," a poem about some birds—
Thrushes, finches, nightingales—who before they assumed the form of
    song
And feathers were just "particles of grain, / And earth, and air, and rain."
I liked the nihilism and the lyricism, then forgot about it,
As I usually do with poems. This week that poem came back to me,
A breath of genius on a tiny, human scale, by contrast with the
Strenuous heroics of high modernism and the mathematical sublime
That have now become a visionary ideal no one aspires to anymore,
Because it can't—it can't what? I'm a sucker for the subtle sentimental,
And I even like it, though I disapprove. I wouldn't say Miss Heaton
Won, and yet I'm moved, without wanting to be moved and against my
    better
Judgment. Of course the way I write is different (so I like to think),
But a pernicious continuity keeps creeping in. Still, I want to
Keep that tiny flame alive, to keep insisting on the difference, even if
The difference may be no more than insouciance with a slight
Heightening at the end, as if Thomas Hardy were sipping a martini.

LITTLE GUYS WHO LIVE HERE

Speaking of cats, when was the last
time you spoke to one, calling it by its name?
— John Ashbery

I sing the cat. Or rather, I sing the small
Animals we keep in our houses, of which cats
Are the prime example. Edgar Allan Poe's
Black Cat notwithstanding—that thing with the hot
Breath and burning eyes—they make you feel at home
In your house, which might otherwise feel empty.
I like to wake up to a cat—a white one in my case—
That's helped me make it through the night
By sleeping on a pad (the "Mysterious Purr Padd")
At the foot of my bed, with forays to my side
To "cuddle," if that's the word, and a nose
Like a cold blossom. I used to have two cats:
The eponymous Chester of another poem of mine,
And Douglas, who made Chester miserable.

They loom larger in their absence than their presence,
Once you've become accustomed to their faces.
There isn't much to do but stare at them
And scratch their ears and wait for their kidneys to fail.
Cat mortality may not seem like the stuff of tragedy,
Yet losing something that's become a part of you,
However small, isn't easy, as Diane discovered
After coming home from the vet's for the last time

To "the silence after the viaticum" and an empty house—
Though in my case Douglas was still there, bothered
By the empty carrying case, and a changed cat thereafter.
Of course we project ourselves onto them, just as we
Project ourselves onto each other, but with this difference:
We have "souls," whatever that might mean, while cats are cute,
And in a way "cute" is all they are. "Such a good guy,"
I keep muttering as he snuggles up at 4 a.m., until I no longer
Know what I mean, and it grows cold from repetition.

"I am Lord of all I survey," I think to myself,
Sitting on the deck of my house in the country, before
Coming home to find I haven't been missed at all:
Douglas sitting on his pad, his small, gruff face
Hiding a deep indifference deflating any pretensions
To transcendence or grandiosity, disdainful as the
Dowagers in one of my favorite *New Yorker* cartoons
Emerging from a performance of *Murder in the Cathedral*:
"*Such* a disappointment. And from the author of *Cats!*"

MELANCHOLY OF THE AUTUMN GARDEN

IN MEMORIAM ROBERT DASH

The driveway to the winter house looks like that
Driveway in *Dead of Night* that leads back to a past
It started out from. I started going out there
In 1974, pre-Jitney: I'd take the train, and usually
I'd run into fellow travelers: Marjorie, or Bill and Willy,
Everyone went out there then. We'd linger around the table
Gesturing at reading the *Times*, planning long walks
And looking forward to the cocktail hour(s).
Darragh was always there, the window frames were white,
The garden was subdued, then it exploded into color,
Purples and pastels around the windows. "You've ruined it"
Said Peter Schjeldahl, and that was it for him. Aladar
Came out in zippers and black leather: "Aladar,
You look just like a purse!" It was the funniest thing
I'd ever heard, which shows you just how giddy
The whole thing was, and why it couldn't last: drunken
Tedium amidst a beauty fashioned from the mind
As much as from the hand and dirt, and the beauty remains.
In time the others drifted one by one away, leaving me
To keep the flame alive, a solitary remnant.
The garden remains outwardly unchanged while changing
With the seasons and the years, beginning with the gentle greens
Of spring, then summer's colors, then warm
Autumn tones, until in mid-November it becomes inert.

*

"And we were drunk for month on month"
(Pound, *Cathay*), and look at where it leads: dialysis
Interminable, that's so excruciating one can faint.
We talked about Mabel Mercer: "All in all /
It was worth it." Was it really? Yes, of course it was,
But what the songs all try to say defies analysis:
There's no such thing as the completely wasted life,
Just lives of varying degrees of opacity and transparency,
Through which the limits of the visible appear.
Instead of years, their real measure is the underlying
Rationale, so hard to articulate, that no one understands,
Though it shows through. I remember walking through the garden
Without any clue beyond its beauty. There was something
Marjorie wanted me to say, and now I can't remember what it was—
Maybe something about gardens over time, who knows?
In spring it's open to the public, but now the view is mine alone,
Taking in the trees with no leaves left, the enclosure with its stubble,
Swaths of gray on gray, the simple placard reading Closed.
It's there for all to see, and yet its meaning lies beneath it or beyond it,
In the fantasies of its creator, which is to say, nowhere at all.
I digress, I acquiesce, I conjure what I want to see from nothing—
That's the way art works. It sounds like fantasies fulfilled,
And yet it's more a record of the things discarded on the way
To a mild November morning, watching the skull beneath the skin,
Or better still, a carapace from which the mortal flesh is gone.
The beauty is what's left. It doesn't make any sense, but there it is.

DOROTHY DEAN

I thought it was starting, and
In retrospect, I suppose it was. *Domes*
Won the Frank O'Hara Award (which killed it off),
And so to celebrate I bought a new green mackinaw
From L.L. Bean and headed for New York. I stayed at
John's, had lunch with an indifferent editor from Columbia U.P.
And hung around with friends. There was a party in a loft
Somewhere downtown—an exhibition of a hundred 2x2-inch
Paintings by George Schneeman, $25 each—and though I
Went there with a friend, I spent the whole night talking to a small
Black woman in a tailored dress who'd majored in philosophy at Harvard,
Where she'd studied Wittgenstein and Aristotle with my own advisor
Rogers Albritton—whom of course we talked about, along with
    Wittgenstein
And art and whether Wittgenstein was gay (such innocent days!).
She said there was a book that clinched the case, we swapped addresses
And I bought a painting and went back to John's, where Robert Dash
And Darragh Park, resplendent in tuxedos from the opera, were on
    display.
I passed around my tiny painting of some laundry on a clothesline.
"So he does have talent," John opined. It was an inauspicious meeting:
When we met again, Bob said that at the time they'd thought I was
(Despite that splendid mackinaw) another downtown bum.

Dorothy Dean turned out to be a minor figure in the Warhol
And *New Yorker* worlds. We carried on a desultory correspondence
For a few years, which included the book she claimed "spilled the gay
    beans

On Wittgenstein," but which it turned out I had read. Now and then
I'd come across her name: on Lou Reed's *Take No Prisoners* where he
Channels Lenny Bruce ("We call her Tiny Malice, Dorothy Dean");
In a show of photographs of Max's Kansas City, where she'd bar the
    door;
As a footnote to my fascination with George Trow, who eulogized her
After she died of cancer in Colorado, where she'd moved in the eighties,
When she couldn't take New York anymore; in a poem of Robert
    Creeley's.
It didn't amount to anything, yet that's where time is measured—
At the intersections of your life with someone else's. Some of them
Are singular, some of them, like mine with Bob's and Darragh's, reoccur
Until somebody dies. You set out with a promise and a wish,
And live in them until the wish and its fulfillment start to seem routine
And the anecdotes begin, the moments that become life stories,
Like that evening over forty years ago I spent with Dorothy Dean.

I realize that almost everybody in this poem is dead now,
Tiny figures flickering through time. At a party at Poets House
Last May I saw a wonderful exhibition of some paintings
Of George Schneeman's of a bunch of poets with their clothes off.
Ron Padgett had co-organized the show, and he recalled that
Night of tiny paintings back in 1972. It was at Holly Solomon's loft,
He told me, and we talked about how they were made with Magic
    Markers,
Which couldn't take the sunlight. "If you bought one and just put it in a
Drawer it was *OK*," he said; "otherwise, in a few years it was gone."
That's what happened to mine: it went from Cambridge to Milwaukee,
Where my son was born, then to a house in Whitefish Bay, where I built
    a study

With a lot of bookshelves, propped it up and looked at it from time to
    time.
I want to resist the urge to sermonize: these connections never occurred
    to me
Until I started writing this, but that's how poetry carries you away.
I looked at it as long as I could see it, but it's gone now, like that house
And the backyard I could ponder from my study. I write in real time,
But the time I write about exists in my imagination, where I used to live
When I was starting out along the road to nowhere, following my
Reflection in the mirror of the future, watching my painting with its
    image
Of some laundry on a clothesline getting fainter and fainter each year;
And by the time Dorothy Dean died it had disappeared.

TULSA

*Always treat humanity, whether in yourself or in another
person, as an end in itself, and never simply as a means.*
—Kant

It wasn't just the slaughter—though proportionally it
Exceeded all our other wars combined—but what prefigured it
And what it brought about. There was the cotton gin
That gave the South a one-commodity economy
It needed slaves to run. And slavery required power,
Political power, to perpetuate itself, and power depended on
New slave states to sustain it, so that when its grandiose fantasy
Of Manifest Destiny—a Caribbean empire absorbing Mexico and Cuba—
Collapsed by 1861, there wasn't anything left to do but secede.
It's sickening to read the rationales, because they cut so close. Mississippi:
"Our position is thoroughly identified with the institution of slavery—
The greatest material interest of the world. Its labor supplies the product
Which constitutes by far the largest and most important portions
Of commerce of the earth. These products are peculiar to the climate
Verging on the tropical regions, and by an imperious law of nature,
None but the black race can bear exposure to the tropical sun.
These products have become necessities of the world,
And a blow at slavery is a blow at commerce and civilization."
Georgia: "Because by their declared principles and policy
They have outlawed $3,000,000,000 of our property." Texas:
"That in this free government *all white men are and of right
Ought to be entitled to equal civil and political rights*;
That the servitude of the African race, as existing in these States,

302

Is mutually beneficial to both bond and free, and is abundantly authorized
And justified by the experience of mankind, and the revealed
Will of the Almighty Creator, as recognized by all Christian nations."

After a desultory start the carnage began in earnest, with standing charges—
The strategy Napoleon had used—into the teeth of modern ordnance
Scattering brains and blood and shattered bones across the open fields,
Until supplanted by the trenches that looked out upon the graves of WWI.
Sometimes the history of a war obscures the meaning of the war:
Behind the strategies and battles—Antietam and Gettysburg of course,
But also those whose names have vanished into books or onto Wikipedia,
Like Peebles' Farm or Philippi or Darbytown or Hoover's Gap—
The unconcluded narrative continued to unfold, conceived
In an original sin no ordinary victory or surrender could erase.
So when that victory finally came and the South gave up,
It was outwardly abolished, and the economic order it sustained
Went with the wind; but the souls of those who wrote those rationales
Remained unvanquished. As the bickering began, fatigue set in
And Reconstruction foundered. The Redeemers persevered,
The White League and the Red Shirts' organized campaigns of terror
Culminated in the Mississippi Plan of 1875, when the besieged
Republican electorate was shot or forced to flee, and Grant,
Fretting about Ohio, declined to intervene. The plan became a model
For the other states—South Carolina signed on too—until rendered
    obsolete
By the Compromise of 1877—the "Corrupt Bargain"—when in return
For the presidency, Rutherford B. Hayes agreed to pull all federal troops
From the South, which became, in effect, a separate nation after all.

*

That's the history part. I guess it's cynical and open to dispute:
There's the legend of the Lost Cause, that romanticized the way of life
The war destroyed, and Whiggish history, in which whites somehow
    forgot
"That blacks were creating thriving middle classes in many states of the
    South."
In 1999 I flew to Tulsa for a literary festival. There was the small city's
Usual downtown whose best days were behind it, and Oral Roberts
    University's
Enormous praying hands that pointed straight at heaven. The people
Who'd invited me showed me the sights (including those gigantic hands),
And during lunch one day described the riots that occurred in 1921.
There was a vibrant black community in a part of town called Greenwood
(One of those thriving middle classes, I suppose), so prosperous with its
Banks and businesses and homes that it was called "the Negro Wall
    Street."
On Memorial Day there was an incident in an elevator in a downtown
    building
That involved a young white woman and a young black man, who was
    jailed
On suspicion of assault. A white crowd gathered, incited by an editorial
In the *Tulsa Tribune* egging on a lynching. Skirmishes ensued,
And then at last a huge white mob stormed into Greenwood, shooting
Indiscriminately, burning stores and businesses and houses, while
    biplanes
From an airfield near town, left over from WWI, dropped firebombs
And fired at people on the ground, until the Negro Wall Street lay in ruins.
No one really knows how many died—hundreds probably, and thousands
    wounded.
There's a modest monument today where Greenwood used to be,

But for over half a century the Tulsa Race Riot simply disappeared from
  history:
The copies of the *Tribune* with the editorial are missing from its archives
And the archives in the capitol; the riot itself went missing from the
  school
And history books, not just in Oklahoma and the South, but
  everywhere;
And there were never reparations. What flabbergasted me, beyond the
  riot itself,
Was the fact of its effacement, and the underlying explanation.
Dick Rowland—that was the young man's name—was just a stand-in
For the real cause: the black community's continually accumulating
  wealth,
That made its partial ownership of the oil companies that composed
The city's soul almost inevitable, but which was unacceptable. And so
  the
Pent-up anger was unleashed, and the worst episode of racial
Violence in the country's history vanished completely from its past.

In metaphysics and philosophy of language there's a view that holds
That if you want to know what something is, ignore what people say
  about it—
Look instead at where it came from. So much of what has plagued our
Politics for centuries now—the distrust of reason and the common good,
  of the ideal
Of justice; the obsession with the perfidy of government, a base
  conception of the social order—
Descended from the original sin of slavery and the desperate struggle to
  maintain it,
Before taking on a life of its own. "There goes the South for a generation,"

Johnson said as he signed the Civil Rights Act, though that was optimistic.
    The rhetoric
Of freedom floats upon the surface of a dark, unspoken dream of
    restoration,
Of a way of life that never actually existed, nurtured by a long forgetting.
The auction blocks and firebombs are gone, yet a straight line runs from
Charleston through Tulsa to today, and though the terms have changed,
The colors too—red and blue instead of black and white—the same
    resentments
And divisions linger, only now without the purpose that sustained them—
As though a nation had retained its sense of grievance, but lost its cause.
Sometimes I think I brood too much on these divides, but then I listen
    to the radio
Or watch TV and feel the hopelessness return. It's strange how anything
    as abstract
As the failure of some quaint ideal of human reciprocity, of the recognition
Of ourselves in others, could reverberate so long, and yet it has. I used to
Think philosophy and history didn't matter in the greater scheme of
    things:
That they were too remote from people's lives to make a difference,
As though the past were just another idle argument we kept repeating,
Without remembering what made it what it is. What it is
Is all around us, however difficult to see. And so the war goes on
In forms we can't quite recognize—accommodating children
Of an old obscenity still living in its lengthening shadow, in its shade.

IN THE LOUVRE

How many crucifixions and bambini do I have to see
To realize these illustrations of the religion I was raised in
Aren't remotely true, as untrue as all those icons of mythology,
The statues in the basement—Venus with her missing arms,
Some satyrs, even Seneca, a man without transcendent qualities,
Gaunt and doomed as Jesus? How many pictures do I have to study
With a feigned enthusiasm till the whole thing feels like a scam
Facilitated by the greatest painters painting has ever known?
How many hordes of people studying them with comprehension
And sympathy do I have to look at till they start to seem like pagans
"Suckled in a creed outworn"?
                                              And yet I love the painting of St. Anne
With Mary and her baby on her lap. Freud argued that that smile,
Like Mona Lisa's in the gallery across the hall, was Leonardo's mother's,
Which you can make of what you choose, depending on your view of
      Freud.
Myths come and go and from a distance feel the same—strange icons
Of a "madness to explain" an unfamiliar world that passeth understanding
And never ends. From faith to superstition to regret: what started
As a screed becomes an elegy for a life deprived of illusions, a lament
For a certainty I thought I had but probably never did, of something
Beyond mere being. Why did I believe it, if I ever did?

CHAPPAQUIDDICK

I hate believing I grew up in a country
Better than the one I live in now. We were vaguely
Middle class: my mother was a schoolteacher,
My father a Navy NCO, a former concert violinist

Who cracked up—a "nervous breakdown"
As they called it then—when I was in the eleventh grade.
Sputnik woke the nation up, money poured in,
The San Diego schools were great, I played the clarinet,

Ran track, won science fairs and then went off to college
In the East, which I imagined would be paradise,
And indeed it was: the country turned out to be green
Instead of brown and tan, New York was new,

The rich were interesting and smart instead of just obscene,
And some of that enchantment trickled down to me.
It didn't last. There was Vietnam of course, but even then
There seemed to be a way to get it right: decency

And common sense, the individual life fulfilled
Within the confines of a common good.
People could create themselves, then finally retire,
The air felt full of possibilities deferred

But realized eventually, the national narrative
Was still in progress, one in which each person's life
Pursued a course that led from infancy to age.
It doesn't really matter whether all of this was true—

It seemed to be, then that perception changed.
When did the page turn and the past turn into paradise?
I remember watching TV shows about the future as a miracle,
With supersonic trains and flying cars and towers

Climbing to the sky. It's a disaster movie now,
A Depression-era song about ambition realized, and gone:
"I built a tower to the sun." I remember those towers
To the sun, and the trains that raced against time.

* * *

I travel a lot, I age, my mood and outlook change.
This week I came to see my granddaughter in Nashville
For the second time, big eyes and bald and smiling
In her Exersaucer with bright blocks and rings and a plastic fish.

On Saturday we went to Carnton Plantation, the site
Of the Battle of Franklin, the bloodiest encounter of the Civil War:
Two thousand dead in five hours, with the house turned into a hospital
And thirty or forty to a room, and stacks of amputated limbs.

Initially the dead were buried in an open field of shallow graves,
Their arms and legs protruding from the ground. Eventually
The village built a proper cemetery, with cypress trees protecting
Rows of regular stone blocks and Baby Lauren in her stroller.

In retrospect the battle was gratuitous: the war was lost,
The military part at least. Nashville is a new Milwaukee, cities
Situated at a confluence of the nation's economic winds:
Prosperity that flowed from immigration and industry and beer,

Followed by cheap labor and the drift of capital from there to here.
That's what the war was actually about: slavery was its cause,
But slavery was unsustainable—it was simply too egregious to endure.
It wasn't race that mattered, it was human property, and property is
    colorless,

Labor fungible—it's not important how it looks or sounds,
As long as it produces and shuts up: skyscrapers going up, restaurants,
Walmarts, football stadiums, neighborhoods that used to be slums
Suddenly sprouting boutiques, people anxiously content, and no real
    future.

I imagine the worst, because the truth is difficult to see.
Lauren, John and Annie, people like me are all going to be fine
(Though I'll be dead), But who'll keep it all? To ask that question
Is to answer it: as we drove past the new Nissan headquarters,

Silver in the sun, I thought about Milwaukee and Detroit
And how they're nobody's fault, because the question reaches back
To the poem of the past, and the dying fall of one last ode
To the Confederate dead, resting in victory beneath the cypress trees.

                              * * *

Sometimes there isn't any explanation for what happened,
Or the explanation is unsatisfying, since it rules out the possibility
Of a different outcome, of things turning out other than they did.
That's when the mind turns to fantasies and paranoia: we *want* them

To be different, as of course they would be but for—for *what?*
The assassinations? Altamont? For Charles Manson? Last month
Diane and I were on Martha's Vineyard, ground zero for the benign rich
I used to love, and in a way still do: there used to be a balance

Between civilization and its discontents, but then that balance
Altered, or continued only intermittently, in small pockets
Of privilege where wealth assumes a human scale. I read my poems,
We ate lobster rolls and drove around the island where they filmed *Jaws*,

Past Inkwell Beach, through Oak Bluffs and the Gothic cottages
Where Methodists once waited on the ending of the world, which
    didn't end.
The world never ends—what ends are explanations of the way it is.
I didn't know where Chappaquiddick was—a part of Martha's Vineyard

It turned out. I remember 1969, and how America was poised between
A recent past already turning into history, and a future that, in theory
    anyway,
Remained open. Nixon had finally got elected, but it didn't have to last—
We could still get back to where things started to collapse, and make it
    work.

I didn't care what shape it took, as long as it resumed the right direction.
I barely read the story in the *Times*, for there were other possibilities,
But one by one they fell away and 1972 became a debacle. True, there was
Watergate, but that was a holding action, as the country changed in ways

I could hardly see. I remember reading *V.* in college, a novel
About a search for something to explain a century, or simply someone's life.
Explanations like that don't exist: we harbor them because they're easy,
And because reality is numb. We took the ferry across a channel

Narrow enough to swim, we walked along a beach that dropped off
Steeply into Nantucket Sound. It was all gone: the party and its aftermath,
The lighted houses they passed on the way to the bridge,
The Oldsmobile that skidded off Dike Road and into Poucha Pond.

E.H.

Sometimes I stand in the middle of the floor,
Not going left, not going right.
—Stephen Sondheim

I like to get drunk and I like to write.
I search for ways in and can't find them,
But that doesn't mean they're not there. What isn't
There is the life between the words, the life that existed
Beyond the words, the life I don't have anymore.
In Michigan the feelings soaked the page,
Yet now they seem diminished in the telling
And no longer in our time, no longer of our place,
But in another country, one of an imagination
Anchored in a style; no longer in the stream
Or swamp, where the fishing was tragic.

I (whichever *I* this is) saw *Follies* last year.
The Weismann Girls come back to stand for what they were
And aren't anymore, in a theatre slated for demolition.
Sally is a prisoner of her rage and imagination,
Pining for the magic of what might have been
Until the spell breaks, leaving her alone on stage
Amid the shards of her illusions. As she looks around
For what she is, all she can find is her age:
"I'm forty-nine. That's all I am."

*

312

Why do I get so angry? Why do I assume
The characters I love, the characters I love and hate?
There's a corruption from which I've never recovered
That diminishes me each day, until I can't tell which I am
Anymore, the mask or the face. The boat in Havana:
Last time was the last time. The stirring begins each night
And continues through the day here in a home that isn't home,
With Michigan far away, the *finca* far away, alone
In the vestibule in the early morning light, imagining
The feeling of cool steel against my forehead
And the sound of two drawers slamming.
I'm sixty-two. That's all I am.

AGAINST IMMORTALITY

Yes, the late night jazz, great sex and all
The human shit defining what we are:
Par for the course. I dwell instead
On minutiae, on little highs defining days
In need of definition: the package on the porch,
The email, the unexpected phone call.
These trivialities provide direction
And a sense of purpose to the small world
Each of us inhabits for a while
Until its time is finished, and it ends.
I know it feels like something to regret,
Yet why would anybody *want* to be immortal?
Immortality isn't what it used to be: the literary version
Comes too late to do you any good, and as for the immortal
Soul, what would it be *like* to lie awake for all eternity,
Without anything ever changing? Give me a break,
It seems to say: return me to the small world I remember,
Where there were surprises and disappointments
And I'd wake up each morning wondering what to do,
And to the fear of death. It energizes everything,
This terrible feeling of being just about to fall,
This terrifying feeling of contingency. Instead it
Offers you the life I'm desperate to escape:
The relief from care, from wanting life to change
For better or for worse; the sitting still.
  Shantih shantih shantih.
No packages, no emails, no phone calls.

FEAR AND TREMBLING

I had to read it the summer before I left for college.
I had a job running a miniature merry-go-round
With dinky airplanes instead of horses, across the street
From the zoo and the natural history museum,
Where I'd read a book that eventually changed my life,
Although I didn't realize it then. It was all about
Not being sure and being sure. It was about the sun of faith
Obscured by the cloud of not knowing. It was about being great.
And after fifty years I'm reading it again, and after fifty years
I'm back in San Diego for my high school class's fiftieth reunion,
Herbert Hoover High School '63. If you had told me then
What I'd be doing now or who I'd be I wouldn't have believed you—
Time is unimaginable until it passes, like the individual life
With which it coincides. And as for God, I didn't believe it then,
And yet it still made sense to me, and doesn't now. It was a metaphor
For being free, since listening to God meant listening to yourself.
A life is made up out of everything it can and can't imagine,
Had and didn't want, wanted and couldn't have—all of it there
In the yearbook for God to see. I wear a name tag with my
Picture circa 1963, carry a drink and wander around the lobby
Of the Lafayette Hotel, glancing down to place each face
Before moving on to the next one, staring into a hotel mirror
At the image of that distant boy who turned out to be me.

Maybe I make too much of things. Kierkegaard did,
Hung up in a no-man's-land between sacrifice and murder,
Between morality and mystery, conjuring up possibilities

Where there were none to see. My Moriah is a fantasy
Of living in the present, of inhabiting the interval
Between the settled past and the illusion of the future,
Which keeps receding. The tale may be superstitious bullshit,
Yet what resonates is the absence of anxiety, the sense
Of purpose, the uncertainty. Greatness is the underlying theme,
But it's invisible: greatness is the absolute, and it remains unknown.
I know the story that came true is not the one I set about to write,
Though it's the one I meant, the one I learned in high school.
Standing around a swimming pool, listening to pre-Beatles rock and roll,
Then flying back across the continent to tell my tale to anyone
Who'll listen: it's complete except for the conclusion,
Which remains unwritten, since it's inconceivable. What's left
Is wonder, wonder and waiting, canvassing the possibilities:
Respite or catastrophe, anonymity or validation—the abrupt angel,
The finality, the stayed hand; the ram caught in the shrubbery.

THE TENDERNESS OF MATHEMATICS

God created the integers, all else is the work of man.
—Leopold Kronecker

He didn't do even that, since he doesn't exist,
And yet they're there: 0, 1, 2, 3 dot dot dot
Ad infinitum. And if Frege was right
(And certainly he was), they descended from
The basic principles of thought, from what we know
If we know anything at all. And yet they constantly surprise:
From out of nowhere number theory gets reflected
In the properties of automorphic forms, the distribution
Of the primes seems like the distribution of the stars
In their indifference to us, and the Eightfold Way,
That leads from Plato's paradise to here, starts out as idle
Speculation, combing through some symmetry groups,
Until the quarks pop out and bathe us in the world.

How can something so abstruse and abstract feel so close
And be so far away? They "force themselves upon us,"
Gödel remarked of the axioms of set theory, and he was right:
Like some watcher of the skies | When a new planet
Swims into his ken, we seem to see the units rearranged
Before our eyes, as what had been implicit all along
Suddenly seems clear. It doesn't happen in life, in real life,
Yet mathematics is a part of life. In high school
I thought I'd proved a theorem about perfect numbers.
The proof contained a fallacy, but for a week or so

I felt like stout Cortez upon his peak in Darien.
The dream of mathematics is of an underlying order
We invented without knowing it, waiting there
Just out of reach, waiting to manifest itself
And for its truths to intrude upon a consciousness
Asleep in its dream, asleep in no one's dream.

LA DURÉE

Proust read Bergson, then he wrote his poem.
I thought if I read Bergson too I'd figure out a way
To say what I've been gesturing at all my life
Without success: *la durée*, duration, time,
My own time, by which I mean your own time too.
I don't know why: the days go by without event,
Resembling one another in the main and in the details,
Each remaining individual in its moment as it
Disappears. The gray day dawns and turns to snow
Accumulating on the cars and on the parking lot
Below my window, other cars roll by along the street
I can see from my desk, while Henri Bergson floats adrift
On confusions about quantity and quality, and I—
I go on reading. Chapter Two: riffings about numbers
By a man who gave up mathematics for philosophy
Too soon, and missed what they'd discovered—
Numbers aren't constructed out of space or human time,
But from a pure idea of order at some Key West of the mind
Beyond duration and experience, where they last forever.
It's a great idea, yet we live in time, and here Bergson is right:
Each moment represents a whole—a whole of *what?* It's
There I start to lose him, as he wonders off into peculiar notions
Of succession, space and time—I want to throw his book against the
Wall as Wittgenstein did whenever he read Hume. The whole
Has got to be a life, an ordinary, individual life, a singular
Existence rounded with a sleep, contained in its entirety in every
Moment, like a pageant bathing in the light of an eternal now.

Sometimes I don't believe a word I say, and then remember why:
I think that everyone's as vexed by time as I am, and because I do
I grab whatever rhetoric comes my way. Of course there's
Something to be said for reticence and tact, but also something to be
Said for passionate abstraction, and for letting contradictions flow
Before relaxing back into reflection and the present tense
And nothing new to say. The poetry of life feels inexhaustible,
But it advances haltingly, besieged by second thoughts
And doubts—basking in the present, then returning to the past
For substance; wandering out into the open, then retreating
Back into the soul's small room; while all the while
Attempting to articulate a single thought constructed out of
Two opposing ones: that life is little; and that life is all.

I don't think this is Bergson: his duration isn't time at all,
At least not time as I conceive it—his duration is a tune
Played by sensations melting into one another to compose a life.
That's what perplexes me in Proust: that those involuntary
Memories awakened by a cookie or the paving stones of Venice
Coalesce into a swoon that lasts three thousand pages.
He thinks everything exists at once, and nothing vanishes
In the chaos of society and sex, or in the small delights
Of coffee and a newspaper; that time returns us to ourselves;
That time restores the flavor of those hours that flourished once
And still survive within the confines of a little phrase.
Bergson: "Pure duration is the form which the succession
Of our conscious states assumes when our ego lets itself *live*."
I just don't get it: my experience of time is so confined,
So limited to *now*. Instead of ranging back and forth
Across successive years, I occupy the span of my attention,

Like a mirror that reflects itself and thus exhibits nothing.
This morning in the *Times* there was a piece about an exhibition
At the Morgan on *Swann's Way*. It quoted from an elegant
Notebook Jacques Bizet's mother gave to Proust: "Should it be a novel,
A philosophical essay, am I a novelist?" Is this a poem, an essay,
Or another form of exercise in time, which after all is what poems are?
It's what I think, or want to say: time can't be pictured or described,
But what those accidental memories, so trivial and insignificant
In themselves, provide is the experience of pure duration, of an interval
Between what happened once and now that measures what we are
And makes us human—not a life recaptured, but a life defined.
Perhaps that *is* what Bergson meant to say, when you abstract away
From all the rhetoric and fallacies: that *la durée* is just the form
A life assumes in retrospect, or that emerges in the contours of a poem.
There's a Fitzgerald story, "The Curious Case of Benjamin Button,"
Whose ending always moves me. The protagonist is born old,
A seventy-year-old baby, and his life develops in reverse:
A successful hardware business, marriage and a child, the charge up
San Juan Hill, then Harvard football, prep school, an inexorably
Diminishing adolescence, immaturity and infancy, as he ages backwards
Into birth and nonexistence. It's narrated in Fitzgerald's characteristic
Clipped romantic style and made a so-so movie. What haunts me
Is the blankness at the end, the rounding sleep. Of course that sleep
Encompasses both ends, but since our own lives ramble on
From day to day and line to line, their end is open and uncertain
And their contours indistinct. But this one ambles backwards
Towards an end that always lies conspicuously in view,
So you can grasp it as a limited totality, and trace its shape.

*

All this is written from a single point of view, my own,
Since that's how time presents itself to me. But real time,
Objective time—the time of history, prehistory and cosmology—
Is something Bergson didn't understand, and I don't either,
Even though I live in it. "Lift your head, look out the window"—
Standard exhortations to forget about yourself and breathe,
And I agree with all of them, and still I don't know what to do.
Love, of course, and sex, but they confine you to yourself
In a kingdom of two, which is what I'm trying to transcend.
Physics helps: a vision of the world beyond appearance
As it is in itself and not from anyone's particular perspective,
Measured by the clocks of mathematics that preceded our
Existence and continue ticking after everyone has gone.
That vision may be one more insubstantial pageant,
Or simply too abstract and literal to actually believe. Maybe
The better way is simply to remain indifferent, but again,
It's one thing to propose it and another thing to see it through.
I remember one time when the feeling of my own existence faltered,
About a year after I'd settled in Milwaukee. I was in a Kmart
Parking lot—a local version of the paving stones of Venice—
And couldn't understand why I was there or what had brought me there.
I fell into a mild depression that persisted for a year or so
And dissipated, leaving me as I am, and as I've been for forty years.
There may be various ways to organize one's story, structuring it
By place-names or by people or by poems, instead of incidents
And years, yet all of them seem equal in the end. A life's
Partitions are internal to it, and of no significance beyond its course.
I can live with that: my own time represents the world to me,
Although I realize it isn't real time at all—and so what?
It keeps me going, incident by incident, chapter by chapter,

Waiting on a denouement that keeps receding into the fog
Of the future, and meanwhile living in a present illuminated
By the glow of the past, and in its shade. This has been a
Poem about time, but see how much of it is visual and spatial,
Just as Bergson said. I didn't read the chapter on free will,
But I can guess at it: we have it, of course, thanks to an obscure
Philosophy. Sometimes a single idea is enough—*la durée*,
Whatever it might mean. I think I live it every day,
Waking every morning to the next episode of a narrative
Whose origin lies beyond the reach of memory, whose
Conclusion is unwritten and whose logic is the free
Association of sensations and desires, governed by appetites
Even in extremis—like Proust, at the end of his duration,
Sending out for a peach, an apricot and iced beer from the Ritz.
I'm hungry. I think I'll get a hamburger at Dr. Dawg.

COVERS BAND IN A SMALL BAR

They make it feel like yesterday,
Which is the whole idea: another dateless
Saturday in the basement of Charter Club,
Drinking beer and listening to a Trenton covers band
Play Four Tops songs: "Sugar Pie, Honey Bunch"
"It's the Same Old Song." They occupied my mind
In 1966 through dinner with Robbie at Del Pezzo, later
In the Vassar Club and on a cruise around Manhattan
For Peter Mahony's parents' wedding anniversary.
My tastes "evolved": more Stax, less Motown,
Then the Velvet Underground and IQ rock—
God, I was a snob. And now Lou Reed is dead
And I'm sitting here in the Art Bar in Milwaukee,
Long past my usual bedtime—*I don't stay out late,*
Don't care to go / I'm home about eight, just me
And my radio—listening to my favorite songs again,
Hearing them as though for the first time? Not at all:
They're too familiar, I'm too preoccupied with them,
Even though the flesh is still willing—swaying
Slightly at the table, nodding up and down
To the memory of "Sugar Pie, Honey Bunch,"
To the melody of "Pale Blue Eyes."

THE AGE OF ANXIETY

       isn't an historical age,
But an individual one, an age to be repeated
Constantly through history. It could be any age
When the self-absorbing practicalities of life
Are overwhelmed by a sense of its contingency,
A feeling that the solid body of this world
Might suddenly dissolve and leave the simple soul
That's not a soul detached from tense and circumstance,
From anything it might recognize as home.
I like to think that it's behind me now, that at my age
Life assumes a settled tone as it explains itself
To no one in particular, to everyone. I like to think
That of those "gifts reserved for age," the least
Is understanding and the last a premonition of the
Limits of the poem that's never done, the poem
Everyone writes in the end. I see myself on a stage,
Declaiming, as the golden hour wanes, my long apology
For all the wasted time I'm pleased to call my life—
A complacent, measured speech that suddenly turns
Fretful as the lights come up to show an empty theater
Where I stand halting and alone. I rehearse these things
Because I want to and I can. I know they're quaint,
And that they've all been heard before. I write them
Down against the day when the words in my mouth
Turn empty, and the trap door opens on the page.

A PRIVATE SINGULARITY

I used to like being young, and I still do,
Because I think I still am. There are physical
Objections to that thought, and yet what
Fascinates me now is how obsessed I was at thirty-five
With feeling older than I was: it seemed so smart
And worldly, so fastidiously knowing to dwell so much
On time—on what it gives, what it destroys, on how it feels.
And now it's here and doesn't feel like anything at all:
A little warm perhaps, a little cool, but mostly waiting on my
Life to fill it up, and meanwhile living in the light and listening
To the music floating through my living room each night.
It's something you recognize in retrospect, long after
Everything that used to fill those years has disappeared
And they've become regrets and images, leaving you alone
In a perpetual present, in a nondescript small room where it began.
You find it in yourself: the ways that led inexorably from
Home to here are simply stories now, leading nowhere anymore;
The wilderness they led through is the space behind a door
Through which a sentence flows, following a map in the heart.
Along the way the self that you were born as turns into
The person you created, but they come together at the end,
United in the memory where time began: the tinkling of a bell
On a garden gate in Combray, or the clang of a driven nail
In a Los Angeles backyard, or a pure, angelic clang in Nova Scotia—
Whatever age restores. It isn't the generalizations I loved
At thirty-five that move me now, but single moments
When my life comes into focus, and the feeling of the years
Between them comes alive. Time stops, and then resumes its story,

Like a train to Balbec or a steamer to Brazil. We moved to San Diego,
Then I headed east, then settled in the middle of the country
Where I've waited now for almost forty years, going through the
Motions of the moments as they pass from now to nothing,
Reading by their light. I don't know why I'm reading them again—
Elizabeth Bishop, Proust. The stories you remember feel like mirrors,
And rereading them like leafing through your life at a certain age,
As though the years were pages. I keep living in the light
Under the door, waiting on those vague sensations floating in
And out of consciousness like odors, like the smell of sperm and lilacs.
In the afternoon I bicycle to a park that overlooks Lake Michigan,
Linger on a bench and read *Contre Sainte-Beuve* and *Time Reborn*,
A physics book that argues time is real. And that's my life—
It isn't much, yet it hangs together: its obsessions dovetail,
As the private world of my experience takes its place
Within a natural order that absorbs it, but for a while lets it live.
It feels like such a miracle, this life: it promises everything,
And even keeps its promise when you've grown too old to care.
It seems unremarkable at first, and then as time goes by it
Starts to seem unreal, a figment of the years inside a universe
That flows around them and dissolves them in the end,
But meanwhile lets you linger in a universe of one:
A village on a summer afternoon, a garden after dark,
A small backyard beneath a boring California sky.
I said I still felt young, and so I am, yet what that means
Eludes me. Maybe it's the feeling of the presence
Of the past, or its disappearance, or both of them at once—
A long estrangement and a private singularity, intact
Within a tinkling bell, an iron nail, a pure, angelic clang—
The echo of a clear, metallic sound from childhood,
Where time began: "Oh, beautiful sound, strike again!"

THE SWIMMER

It was one of those midsummer Sundays . . .
—John Cheever

Photo: sitting by the cabin on Lake Au Train
We rented every summer, reading John Cheever,
Then rowing out in a boat after dinner to fish.
The light would turn golden, then start to fade
As I headed home, past a new log dream house
I could see from our porch, and wished I could own.
I was married then and lived in my imagination,
Writing the poems I was sure would make my name
Eventually, and meanwhile waiting out the afternoons
Within the limits of a world that never changed,

The world of stories. I was almost thirty-eight,
With the compulsion to immortalize myself
That comes with middle age and disappointment.
I knew what I imagined and desired, yet didn't know,
For even though desire can delineate the contours
Of a life, its true substance is beyond desire
And imagination, unrecognizable until it's happened.
In seven years the substance of my future changed:
Instead of summers on the lake, I found myself alone
And free, not wanting what I'd wanted anymore,

And happy. Happiness, unhappy people say,
Comes in degrees, and yet it isn't true. The same
Ambitions and desires, the same attachments
And designs can constitute two different worlds—

A world I'd lived in and a world I never knew
Until I entered it, and made it mine. I wrote a long,
Meandering poem on marriage and its aftermath
That argued (if a poem can argue) that it never ends,
But stays suspended in time, like an afternoon
In August in our small cabin, with the television on

And the lake still visible beyond the door.
It's all still there, in that decade out of mind
I never think about anymore, until some moment
In a movie, or in a story I thought I'd read
And hadn't, or read and can't remember
Brings it back, and then I'm thirty-eight again,
The future still uncertain and there for the taking,
Which is what I did, though I didn't know it—
Which doesn't matter now, for though those wishes
Did come true, it wasn't as I'd dreamed them.

"The Monkey's Paw" is a story about three wishes—
The first one a disaster, the second one an unintended
Horror it takes the last wish to dissolve—that ends
On an empty street. My story is not so dramatic,
Yet the ending feels the same: I have the life
I wanted, people know my name, music fills the rooms
Each evening and each day renews the miracle,
And yet it's not the same. The real world can never
Realize a fantasy lived in the imagination,
That only felt like heaven while it wasn't there.

I thought I'd read "The Swimmer" sitting by the lake
Those thirty-something years ago, but when I looked at it
Last week I couldn't remember reading it at all. It's a story

Devastating on its face—an allegory of the dissolution
Of its hero, who on a beautiful suburban afternoon
Sets out for home by way of swimming pools and alcohol.
His quest begins in confidence and gladness, but as its course
Unfolds its tenor starts to change, as the watercolor
Light begins to fade, the air turns colder and he ages visibly,
Until it ends in autumn, darkness and an empty house.

The moral of the allegory is implicit, but it seems to me
More moving read another way—as a reimagining
Of a life from the perspective of disillusionment and age.
It still starts on a summer afternoon, but a remembered one.
Instead of youth and confidence and hope dissolving,
They're already gone, and instead of a deteriorating world,
It's an indifferent one. I feel at home in this amended parable:
It fits the way a story ought to fit, and it even feels true.
Sitting in my house in the country, there isn't much to do
But stare at the trees through the patio doors open to the deck.

It's not the dream house I remember, but at least it's mine,
And at least I'm happy, though I've lately come to recognize
That happiness is not what it's cracked up to be. As for poetry,
Poetry turned out fine, though nobody actually cares about it
In the old sense anymore. That's the trouble with stories—
They need to come to a conclusion and to have a point,
Whereas the point of growing old is that it doesn't have one:
Someone sets out on an afternoon, following his predetermined
Course as all around him summer darkens and the leaves turn sere,
And finally arrives at home, and finds there's nothing there.

New Poems

PROSPECTS FROM THE PALISADES

We're always other people, whoever they are.
I'm grateful to poets' biographies—a genre nearly as
Obsolete as its subjects—for helping me make myself up,
Though with this last one of Wallace Stevens, that
Owl of the Imagination, I hardly have to try,
Just check off the anomalies as the chapters go by:
Pennsylvania, echt deutsch; a minor jock in high school;
Harvard, New York, confusions of the heart; parents estranged
By a marriage; a boisterous temperament; an ovoid shape.

I'm supposed to sound like him, though I don't hear it.
What I hear is an elevated tone, tinctured with death:
The cheerfulness of disillusionment, the exhilaration of No,
The power of the words when you don't believe them anymore
And you're left with them. I like to think I'm clearer,
That I have ideas beyond their sounds, but it doesn't matter.
What matters is the brute presence of the world, the mute response.
Poets come and go and what they see are redoubtable forms of nothing,
Whether from a secluded refuge on the Palisades or an SUV:
An inert blue sky, themselves, these shelves on shelves of clouds.

RURAL CHURCHES

You could stop on your bicycle, remove your cycle-clips
And go inside, after making sure no one's there;
Or you could drive past in your SUV, which is what I do—
Wondering, in either case, if much still happens there

Inside those churches that must have been assembled from kits
An indeterminate number of years ago. Perched on a hill
On Haney Ridge Road against a resonant blue sky,
On a curve on Highway S, on the road to Mt. Sterling,

They're always surrounded by small graveyards
Supporting occasional ghosts, fences and a few flowers.
I read *Wisconsin Death Trip* when I moved here forty years ago:
The death beneath the beauty, behind "the vast obscurity

Beyond the city . . ." I reread *Gatsby* every year,
Basking in its clarity, finding in the balance of its sentences
What I imagine people used to find in rural churches
Once upon a time, when there was still time.

Last week I imagined stopping at one. There would have been
A padlock on the door, but through a window on the side
It would have looked much as another looked to Philip Larkin
When he stopped at it in England sixty years ago:

A tiny altar, matting, seats and hymnals; but no stone,
No organ, the glass in the paned windows clear instead of stained.
Perhaps I'll actually stop at one next time, though I doubt it:
It's not a matter of curiosity, or wanting to go home again,

Though I was brought up in religion. It's the lack of point:
Whatever Sunday morning used to say about salvation,
Art about eternity, poems about ordinary happiness, they're merely
Quaint now, parts of the scenery like abandoned buildings—

As though those preoccupations had become obsolete,
Little chapels of sound, beautiful in their ways,
But tethered to their times. What's left is simply literal:
The blue sky, the flowers, the dead lying round.

POETRY AT TWENTY-ONE

FOR JULIA RICHARDS

I turned twenty-one halfway through my senior year in college,
Which meant I could open a charge account at the liquor store
On Nassau Street, where by May I'd run up a bill in the staggering
Amount of a hundred dollars, which of course I couldn't pay.
You couldn't graduate until you'd settled up your bills
With the local merchants, and since my teetotaling parents
Would, as they now say, "have a cow" if they'd found out, there was
     nothing
I could do but put it out of my mind or resign myself to fate, i.e., pray.

In April I'd read in the unfortunately named Glascock
Poetry Competition at Mount Holyoke, a contest for mostly
Ivy League poets, like David Shapiro from Columbia,
Who'd published a real book before he was old enough to drive.
Everyone (including David) was certain that he'd win,
And yet I did my best, squeezing five or six poems
(Including two sestinas) into fifteen minutes, while he read two.
Next day John Godfrey drove all of us to New York—David and me
And a Mount Holyoke girl who'd fallen under David's spell.
We stopped by his dormitory at Columbia, where I met Keith Cohen
And heard the Velvet Underground for the first time, went out for the first
Real Chinese meal of my life, and then John drove us back to Princeton,
Where a spring party weekend was in full swing on Prospect Street.

I forgot about it. Spring proceeded to its logical conclusion,
With exams, more parties, and the sense of a story winding down.

I wrote my final college poem ("Maps," a poem I still enjoy),
But no solution to my liquor bill dilemma had emerged—until one day
A letter from Mount Holyoke arrived, informing me I'd won the
   Glascock Prize
And enclosing a check for a hundred dollars. (Thirty years later Donald
   Justice,
Who'd been one of the judges, told me "There was this guy who was
   sure he'd win,
And there was you, who was sure he wouldn't, but we preferred your
   poems.")
I was saved, commencement came and went, and here I am. Who says
Poetry makes nothing happen? As Hilary Putnam once remarked
Of philosophy, it may be a backwater, but it's still part of the stream of
   life.
I like to think that poetry always matters in a small way, and sometimes
Even in a big one—as it did that May in nineteen sixty-seven,
When I was twenty-one, it meant the world to me, and it saved the day.

PORTRAIT OF THE POET

Inner turbulence: a good thing
Early on, but then it gets tired.
The play of the passions peters out
Like a dog in its day, leaving a haze
Of humor, a shelf of required
Readings for the recently retired—
Anger spent, as judiciousness prevails
And the Kindly Ones supplant the Furies.

My brother, my double, myself—
Can't you see where this tends?
It tends towards something vanishingly
Small, inviolate and unperturbed, that begins
Where it ends: towards the sense of a life
Brought to life; towards the irreducible
Self waiting there at the center of its world.

IN PRAISE OF PHYSICAL FORMS

. . . something I could touch, touch every way.
—Stevens

FOR WARREN MACKENZIE

Poems are vessels of the mind, volumes
Whose contours trace the vagaries of thought.
Painting, drawing, collage—they're all exercises
In imaginary spaces, as music is an exercise
In time, and life is too. They're immaterial forms
Of being, different ways of making something up,
Felt so deeply you become them while they last.
The figure in the carpet, the phantom in the snow—
They're other forms of unreality, ways of living
In the presence of nothing, from the imaginary
Notes in the air to the writing on the wall.

That's why I'm happy here amidst the pots.
The ethos bothers me—honesty and clay,
Materiality and function—for though I realize
It's the point, it's not what moves me.
What moves me is the fact of their existence,
Of having nothing much to say beyond arguing
For a reality made up of matter and a form
To be looked at, picked up, and then put down.
Take this anagama vessel with some finger-marks
Where it was grasped before the fire finished it:

An object of desire, certainly, yet indifferent to it.
I see it as a proof of an external world—
Like Dr. Johnson trying to refute Berkeley
By kicking a rock—that you can hold in your hands.

PLASTIC SAXOPHONE

I hate authenticity. I don't mean truth
Per se, which is common sense
Plus science. What I dislike
Is the sound of truth without the facts
To back it up, the rhetoric of conviction
Without the underlying ground, the poetry
Of air, of personality—
                              which is why I love jazz:
I love the way its argument develops
As pure sound, in terms that remain unstated
Until the melody comes around again, and it ends.
Ornette Coleman didn't blow up that frame
So much as deepen it, with individual instruments
So palpable they *were* the melody. He bought a plastic
Saxophone out of necessity, then came to adore its sound.
He urged Terry Gross to bring her clarinet to his group
And see what happened (she didn't go). I should
Elaborate these themes, but that would betray the point:
That the logic of creation isn't based on truth,
As understanding is, but on nerve and free association
In the service of a common good, which only reveals itself
In retrospect, as a way of feeling rather than a vision.
When he died last week there was a long obituary
In the *Times* and an old interview on NPR.
He began each answer with "*Well*, . . ."—a mark
Of modesty—followed by an astonishing articulation
Of just what he meant, like his records.

He had a kind mind, a large heart and his music—
A term that seems too narrow—is a testament
To the art of someone who begat the simplest change
Of the century and remained a perfect gentleman to the end.

THE VIOLET HOUR

It's when the eyes and back turn upwards
Towards the evening news, and tempers flare,
And the airwaves are filled with posturing, evasion
And abuse second only to Sunday morning—
Though even there a poetry lurks in the corners:
In allusions and titles, in the adolescent wish
That language and thought might be both better
And true, and in the anger that they aren't.
I wish I knew why people put up with the present,
When the future it prefigures seems so obvious
And wrong and easy to avoid. The burden
Of its song is always Never, the stasis it induces
Is unyielding, as though meant to last forever.

It's also a chic bar in Chicago I've never been to,
Though when we go down there in a couple of weeks
To celebrate her birthday, Diane and I might go there too—
Who knows? It isn't the near future I worry about,
It's the distant one, when I won't exist anymore
And the sound of my voice won't even be a memory.
If the public and the personal make up different worlds,
As any sane person thinks, why even care about the future?
It isn't there the way the present is, and even though
The parts of it I'll live to see might matter to me,
The rest of it is unimaginable, which makes it poetry.

I sit here frowning at the news and staring at the skylight
Above the dining table, paralyzed by the idea of small
Pleasures and Bradford billionaires to come, as time present
And time future come together in the violet hour.

AFTER ALL

"After all," that too might be possible . . .
—John Ashbery

It isn't too late, but for what I'm not sure.
Though I live for possibility, I loathe unbridled
Speculation, let alone those vague attempts
At self-exploration that become days wasted
Trying out the various modes of being:
The ecstatic mode that celebrates the world, a high
That fades into an old idea; the contemplative,
That says *So what?* and leaves it there;
The sceptical, a way of being in the world
Without accepting it (whatever that might mean).
They're all poses, adequate to different ends
And certain ages, none of them conclusive
Or sufficient to the day. I find myself surprised
By my indifference to what happens next:
You'd think that after almost seventy years of waiting
For the figure in the carpet to emerge I'd feel a sense of
Urgency about the future, rather than dismissing it
As another pretext for more idle speculation.
I'm happy, but I have a pessimistic cast of mind.
I like to generalize, but realize it's pointless,
Since everything is there to see. I love remembering
For its own sake and the feel of passing time
It generates, that lends it meaning and endows it
With a private sense of purpose—as though every life

Were a long effort to salvage something of its past,
An effort bound to fail in the long run, though it comes
With a self-defeating guarantee: the evaporating
Air of recognition that lingers around a name
Or rises from a page from time to time; or the nothing
Waiting at the end of age; whichever comes last.

UNNATURAL LIGHT

We prize clearheadedness: saying
What we mean, meaning what we say,
A metavirtue that blows the real virtues away.
Examples abound, but a lot of good they do:
Politics and the cult of authenticity
Disguising base and ridiculous views;
The TV shows I'm stuck with in the gym,
Where people with no discernible occupations
Level with each other; the way we talk to one another,
With simple rudeness offering itself as candor.
I'm not exempt: this clarity of style
Obscures what lurks beneath the surface
Of a juvenile mind whose explanations are too smooth,
Inventing stories and waiting for them to come true.
You'd think the difficulty would be obvious,
But it's not, since it's only visible from far away
And we're too close to ourselves to see what we really are.
Poets like to think their new poems are their best ones,
Though they usually aren't. Poems are mostly
Wishful thinking, especially the dark ones.

THE SIN OF PRIDE

turns out not to be a sin at all, but in the guise
Of self-esteem a virtue; while poetry, an original
Sin of pride for making self-absorption seem heroic,
Apologizes again and shuts the door. O Small
Room of Myself, where everything and nothing fits,
I wish the night would last forever as the song assures,
Though it never does. I make my way not knowing
Where it leads or how it ends—in shocks of recognition,
In oblivion deferred, too little or too late, consumed
By fears of the forgotten and of the truly great. Morning
Brings a newspaper and an ordinary day, the prospect
Of a popular novel, though it's hard to read. I write to live
And read to pass the time, yet in the end they're equal,
And instead of someone else's name the name I hear is mine—
Which is unsurprising, since our stories all sound alike,
With nothing to reveal or hide. How thin our books
Of revelations, the essential poems of everyone
Mysterious on the outside, but with nothing to conceal—
Like the stories of experience I go on telling myself
And sometimes even think are true, true at least to a feeling
I can't define, though I know what I know: of a mind
Relentlessly faithful to itself and more or less real.

TEMPTING FATE

I know it means to take a risk,
But I prefer the semi-pun:
That we're seduced by the idea
Of helplessness—that whatever we do,
Our ends are preordained, and once begun
Our lives proceed to their conclusions
With the impersonal precision of a well-made play.
I dislike drama. Whatever brought me here—
Whatever *left* me here—remains unwritten, waiting
For its masterwork to be completed, when no one
Cares about it one way or another anymore.
What *is* the deep attraction of the fantasy
That everything just happens, nothing is meant,
And whatever you do you're simply what you are?
It isn't anything experience confirms,
But something we're determined to believe:
That instead of equaling the sum of his revisions,
A person amounts to what he leaves, which disappears.

I don't believe a word of it. When on the opposing side
Of the ledger I calculate the years I've spent preparing—
Or really, not preparing—for my fate, all I feel is gladness:
Not for anything I've done or what I am, but for the underlying
Miracle that magnifies my life and let my world begin.
I owe myself to accidents: when in the course of human
Randomness the stars were in alignment or across a crowded
Room two destinies combined, nothing in an eternal sense
Occurred, yet it left me as I am: a ridiculous person

Worried about bills, gasoline mileage, a new car, grateful
For the presence of a present accentuated by sadness,
Moving without deliberation to the measures of his heart.
This cheerfulness (or is it just indifference?) isn't a facade,
And yet it's fragile, prone to crumbling at the dropping of a hat.
Sometimes in the midst of life—in an airplane, standing on a sidewalk,
At home and leafing through a magazine—I suddenly feel alone,
With a sense of sheer contingency, and I feel afraid.

I think rhetoric is glorious, unleashing meanings
That didn't exist before, but I hate its need to make things up.
Take this poem: reading a biography of James Merrill,
I felt inflected by a germ of words. I'm in New York, saw JA
After five whole years, talked about JM, JS, JY, JG,
Without any spirits intervening. DK was angry as usual,
Which made me feel at home. How can anybody live here?
It costs too much, everyone is ugly, everyone is beautiful,
All of them have stories. People don't have stories,
Just lives that no one wants to hear about. I like people
In small doses, but when I look up at the buildings and blue sky,
They're reduced to their initials, which stand for their lives.
What I like are poems with people's names in them,
Where the reality behind those names remains unfinished,
Waiting on that day that never comes, when we pronounce ourselves
And meet one another as we are. Meanwhile we live in abeyance,
Posting brief bulletins to remind us of each other—
Here I am, won't you friend me, don't forget to write—
If only for the sake of someone's sudden recognition
Of someone else, existing in the creases, living far,
Far away, beyond imagination, which is par for the course.
Hope to read about you soon. D, you know who you are.

WALKING BACKWARDS

You notice them on campuses in early April, the maître d's
Of the future showing customers to their tables. It looks so hopeful:
Come join me, realize your dreams here in this library, this gym,
These classrooms where you can study Shakespeare or Peter Drucker

And above all *Begin*. And then of course it peters out: Is *this*
What you wanted to do, how you wanted to live, who you wanted to be?
I'm a sucker for regrets and retrospective disappointments, as in
Merrily We Roll Along, which begins with a tell-it-like-it-is cynicism

And works backwards to an optimism so naive it makes you cry.
Sometimes I think I overdo it. If the point of disenchantment
Is to make it clear how literal life is, and how contingent
Even moments of transcendence are, there should be nothing to fear

From the future, even as the years go by and nothing happens
And one wish supplants another with a dying fall. And there isn't:
Business used to be as dubious a major as history or English,
People muddled through to law school or advertising or Wall Street

And then wondered what had happened. There's something
Comforting about rituals renewed, even adolescents' pipe dreams:
They'll find out soon enough, and meanwhile find their places
In the eternal scenery, less auguries or cautionary tales

Than parts of an unchanging whole, as ripe for contemplation
As a planisphere or the clouds: the vexed destinies, the shared life,
The sempiternal spectacle of someone preaching to the choir
While walking backwards in the moment on a warm spring afternoon.

COGITO REDUX

I know I'm a creation of my brain,
But once that genie escapes its bottle,
It gets to say what's real. *I'm* real,
It says, along with my brain, as the much
Maligned Descartes maintained, and he was right.
Any knowledge we might attain is due to *us*,
The plural of *me*, but I can't claim credit:
It's just that otherwise there'd be nobody there
To figure it out, nobody there to *know*.
It starts out with how things look
To *someone*, and goes on from there
To a tentative conclusion that's consistent
With whatever it explains, with how things *seem*,
With how they seem to me. Appearances
Are perspectival: nothing looks like anything
To no one, which is to say the view from nowhere
Isn't a view at all. We're empiricists in the broad sense
After all, trying to make sense of our experiences
Within the bounds of reason, and if reason leads to nobody,
It's empty. I may be all intuition, but I'm hardly blind:
The things I feel and see are all I have to go on,
And the stories I tell, however fragile,
Force themselves on me as true, as one by one
My friends keep dying. I haven't heard that sentence yet,
But it's a matter of time (everything's a matter of time)
Before my own image starts dissolving. For now

It still glares up at me, like the celebrated frog
At the bottom of the mug from which I drink to celebrate
This proof of my self, unable to stop believing in it
Even as, with studied curiosity, I await its dissolution.

THE RELUCTANT ELEGIST

A gentleman is someone who can play the accordion and doesn't.
—W. H. Auden

I like to sit here and congratulate myself.
"I ask you," I ask myself, "was the light ever better
On the lower meadow?" Mark died a year ago,
Just after I sat here looking at the same light
And thinking of him. I don't recognize poetry anymore—
It seems like people banding together to validate themselves
In the easiest genre to master, and effecting nothing.
The feel for life, the presence that surrounded the page
Like an atmosphere—these seem like souvenirs
Of a different era, when nobody told you what to say
And so you said it. I miss the way it mattered
And the way no matter what was said or who was speaking
There was always more to understand than what there was to see.
It's all noise now, a pervasive background to the days
That remain indifferent to it. I know it's the same fantasy
Everyone peddles, of an eloquent past from which the present fell,
And I know it's an excuse: I'm only truly happy doing *this*,
Which is more and more infrequent. And even that isn't true—
I *believe* in sentences: they make life feel human
Even as it's ending, and even though there's no one listening.
Watch the sunlight dying on the hill: my pleasure
Is to sit here quietly, until a half-remembered
Sense of something tangible returns, and I almost
Feel like singing, however hesitantly, and clear my throat.

SELFIE STICK

To snap yourself from half a life away,
With the City of Lights floating in the background
And a smile frozen on the same face you wore on a day
In 1985 in the garden of Hotel des Marronniers,
The hotel we're staying in now. *On a day*:
What used to be a real time and an actual place
Isn't real anymore, although the person that I'd been
Is still real, and the eternal present I inhabit remains real too,
At least for now. What holds it together is internal to it,
Like the music of the mirror that arises out of nowhere
And continues forever, through the vagaries of adolescence
And middle age and the fear of gradually getting old,
Until it ends abruptly, for no reason, on a random afternoon,
The way a Patricia Highsmith character might die, in a freak fall
On a nondescript street thousands of miles from home.

It didn't happen. But something like it will in time,
And then time ends. Life seems necessary from the inside,
But from the outside it's contingent and terrifying,
With the precariousness of existence written on its face.
I keep waiting for the thing to happen, meanwhile
Holding it at arm's length, keeping it at bay.

THINKING ABOUT DEATH

I am not thinking of Death, but Death is thinking of me.
—Mark Strand

Lucretius has an unconvincing argument
For why death doesn't matter, since I won't exist
When it occurs. No, goes the rejoinder, it does,
For it deprives me of a life I would have had
And probably would have loved—a rejoinder
I find hard to comprehend. It looks at life
As though it's there to lose, like a sense of humor
Or a book, instead of something that eventually has to end,
Although its ending, from the inside, makes no sense.
I am my world. (The microcosm.)—Wittgenstein.
I'm not sure I understand that either, yet it resonates with me:
What ceases to exist isn't the private singularity—
A single consciousness detached from its surroundings—
But a whole milieu with which it coincides, that dies with it.
I remember lying on a couch one Sunday thirty years ago
When this way of thinking about death took hold of me.
I'm a realist philosophically: the world of all that is the case
Is no one's, while the world of my experience is my own.
I can't pretend to find the right emotion: bewilderment or terror,
Fear, a sense of wonderment, regret—they all seem credible
And insufficient, meant for things that happen *in* a life,
Though not its end. Most thoughts of death feel fake:
They focus on the *I*, instead of what that individual *sees*

From its miraculous and commonplace perspective—
Ordinary days that gradually become an open-ended story
In the present, important for the sake of whose it is.
I used to think that all those stories were alike
In everything but their details, and not worth telling.
Now I think they differ in their tone, and tone is everything:
Tone makes their unavoidable conclusions human,
And their narratives without a moral seem to have one.
The thoughts of death that move me aren't articulate—they're
Moments when the self looks in the mirror of its world
And senses that it's going to disappear, in all of its particularity.
I find it hard to get upset about that loss—it's simply *stuff*,
Albeit *my* stuff: breakfast and the morning newspaper, the mail,
The random sounds that find their order as the day goes on,
The faces lingering in a certain light. What's harder
Is the thought that it will all be *gone*. I'm in the country
Closing up my house. An early snowfall lies upon the deck
And meadow where the elm tree used to be—a merely
Temporary loss that time can overcome with other trees that,
Forestalling the inevitable, I'll get to see next spring.
That other loss is permanent, but never comes
Within the lifetime of experience it ends: a totality
That won't be anyone's anymore, unless a perfect word
Might stay the time of its demise . . . which it won't:
No matter how much you cajole it to remain,
It vanishes, along with what perceived it—all those
Minutes, all the shapes that filled them, all those
Nuances of tone, this afternoon's November
Sun that filters through the branches
And the cows and buildings frozen on a hill
In the urine-colored light. They'll be gone too.

ACKNOWLEDGMENTS

The new poems in this book originally appeared in the following publications: *Boston Review* ("Portrait of the Poet"); *Copper Nickel* ("Tempting Fate"); *Cut-Bank* ("English 206"); *Hampden-Sydney Poetry Review* ("Poetry at Twenty-One," "Unnatural Light," "The Violet Hour"); *Kenyon Review* ("Thinking about Death," "Walking Backwards"); *Prelude* ("Plastic Saxophone," "Rural Churches"); *Raritan* ("In Praise of Physical Forms," "The Reluctant Elegist"); *Tin House* ("After All," "Cogito Redux," "Selfie Stick"); and *The Yale Review* ("Prospects from the Palisades"). "The Sin of Pride" appeared on Poem-a-Day, an online feature of the Academy of American Poets. "Thinking about Death" and "Walking Backwards" were republished on the website Poetry Daily.

INDEX OF TITLES AND FIRST LINES

Made in the USA
Monee, IL
18 October 2020